# HOW TO

YOUR SERIOUS STEP-BY-STEP BLUEPRINT

# WRITE

FOR CREATING INCREDIBLY, IRRESISTIBLY,

# FUNNIEST

SUCCESSFULLY HILARIOUS WRITING

How to Write Funniest

Book three of Your Serious, Step-By-Step Blueprint for Creating Incredibly, Irresistibly, Successfully Hilarious Writing

ISBN: 9798652464264

*For the team*

# ALSO BY SCOTT DIKKERS

*How to Write Funny*

*How to Write Funnier*

*Outrageous Marketing: The Story of The Onion
and How To Build a Powerful Brand with No Marketing Budget*

*Welcome to the Future Which Is Mine*

*Trump's America: Buy This Book and Mexico Will Pay for It*

*43: A Portrait of My Knucklehead Brother Jeb (by George W. Bush)*
with Peter Hilleren

*E-Day! The Funniest Screenplay Never Produced*
with Jay Rath

*Our Dumb World*
with the staff of *The Onion*

*Destined For Destiny: The Unauthorized Autobiography of George W. Bush*
with Peter Hilleren

*The Onion's Finest News Reporting, Volume One*
with the staff of *The Onion*

*Our Dumb Century: 100 Years of Headlines From America's Finest News Source*
with the staff of *The Onion*

*You Are Worthless: Depressing Nuggets of Wisdom Sure to Ruin Your Day*

*The Pretty Good Jim's Journal Treasury: The (Even More) Definitive Collection of Every
Published Cartoon*

*Plebes: The Cartoon Guide for College Guys*

*I Finally Graduated from High School: The Sixth Collection of Jim's Journal Cartoons*

*I Feel Like a Grown-Up Now: The Fifth Jim's Journal Collection*

*I Got Married If You Can Believe That: The Fourth Collection of Jim's Journal Cartoons*

*I Made Some Brownies and They Were Pretty Good: The Third Jim's Journal Collection*

*I Got a Job and It Wasn't That Bad: The Second Collection of Jim's Journal Cartoons*

*I Went to College and It Was Okay: A Collection of Jim's Journal Cartoons*

*Commix*
with Kathryn Rathke, Chris Ware, J. Keen, James Sturm, Jay Rath

BOOK **3**  HOW TO WRITE
FUNNY

# HOW TO

## YOUR SERIOUS STEP-BY-STEP BLUEPRINT

# WRITE

## FOR CREATING INCREDIBLY, IRRESISTIBLY,

# FUNNIEST

## SUCCESSFULLY HILARIOUS WRITING

# SCOTT DIKKERS

# TABLE OF CONTENTS

1 : REVOLUTION         13

*Make sure you're on the winning side of the once-in-a-millennium comedy revolution*

2 : READY, FIRE, AIM      19

*Eliminate the number one obstacle to producing the funniest comedy*

3 : CHIMPS      25

*Circumvent your natural instincts to create your best comedy writing*

4 : MYTH VS. REALITY      31

*Resist chasing writers' room myths that result in bad comedy writing*

5 : WHO ARE THESE PEOPLE?      39

*Know your team and what role each member plays to draw out the best in them*

6 : TAKING THE REINS      47

*Know when to lead, follow, or help for the smoothest possible writer meetings*

7 : BEING BOSSY      57

*Lead your team by taking on the most important roll in the writers' room*

8 : LET ME HELP     65

*Take on the second-most-important role in the writers'*
*room to enjoy myriad benefits*

9 : THE MEETINGS     69

*Employ the best system for running a writers' room for*
*smooth, efficient comedy creation*

10 : A UNITED FRONT     83

*Get clarity on the goal of your writers' room to stay*
*focused on the top priority*

11 : THRIVE IN ANY ROOM     91

*Be the best individual writer possible to make the best*
*group possible*

12 : TAKING THE STAGE     97

*Practice running a writers' room to build your*
*leadership skills*

13 : GOING VIRTUAL     103

*Turn your writers' room into a virtual group that can*
*meet any time, any place*

14 : ANOTHER SECRET WEAPON     107

*Harness the most powerful tool in comedy*

15 : NO MORE STAGE FRIGHT     119

*Get the confidence you need to face a crowd and make*
*them laugh*

16 : Go Nuts      129

   *Armed with knowledge, go forth and make great comedy*

Acknowledgments      135

*Find a group of people who challenge*
*and inspire you, spend a lot of time with*
*them, and it will change your life.*

— Amy Poehler

# 1

# REVOLUTION

There's a revolution happening in comedy. Just a few years ago, professional comedy only came from two sources: people who spoke in front of audiences, and people who wrote for big print outlets. This small handful of professionals was the only source for all the mass-media comedy in the world.

It's all different now. Now, everyone is a comedy writer.

Every day hundreds of millions of people post their best jokes on Twitter, and those jokes have the same potential to reach a mass audience as jokes written by seasoned professionals. There are more jokes on Facebook and Instagram, and still more on YouTube, blogs, podcasts, and everywhere else. Everyone in the developed world—billions of people—has access to these platforms and countless others. There's so much comedy available to audiences today that the most ardent fan couldn't possibly consume it in a million lifetimes.

Some of these billions of jokes from non-professionals are pretty funny. Some are *really* funny. These are the jokes that rise to the top of the more-or-less meritocracy of the Internet and go viral.

How can you get your jokes to go viral? How can you get your short pieces or sketches or stand-up videos to tap into this shortcut to mass exposure?

To reverse engineer that kind of success and repeat it, we just have to look at the source of the comedy revolution.

Within the revolution lies the secret to going viral not only once, by sheer luck, but over and over, reaching large audiences consistently with a winning comedy formula, and building a successful comedy brand.

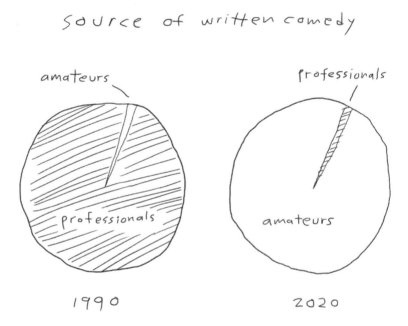

In the first book in this series, *How to Write Funny*, I gave you the first step to finding an audience: master the short one-line joke. By crafting hilarious short jokes, you grab people's attention and compel them to notice your work. If you can continue writing and posting hilarious jokes, audiences come to trust you as a source for quality comedy. In the second book, *How to Write Funnier*, I laid out the best practices for expanding the one-line joke into a sustained piece of comedy like a story, stand-up bit, or sketch. These longer forms of comedy hold the audience's attention beyond the one-line joke, further cementing your bond with them.

If you've read those two books—which you'd be well served to do before you read this one—you're already on your way to rising above the din of the world's millions of would-be comedy writers to capture the attention of a large audience. You're well armed to pierce through the immense tide of comedy competition to become a successful comedy writer.

In this book, you're going to learn how to take things even further. You're going to learn how to make your comedy irresistible.

Comedy can be a lonely pursuit. Comedy writers are often hunkered at their desks in solitude trying to crank out something amusing. Far too many are consumed by anxiety, wondering, "What if I'm not funny?" With the endless barrage of top-notch humor flooding the Internet from these millions of fellow writers, the anxiety becomes a burning fever that can tempt even the best comedy writers to throw up their hands in defeat.

The good news is, you don't have to beat everybody to create something funny, cut through the noise, and get seen. There's a slice of the fan pie, no matter how small, for everyone. And grabbing hold of a small pie positions you nicely to grab another piece and inevitably increase your share.

The task of the modern comedy writer is simple: write the funniest material. Okay—simple to say, but not so simple to do.

At least, not until now. This book contains the secret to maximizing the quality of your humor so it's the funniest.

After writing in solitude and realizing that it's a painful, lonely pursuit, most writers turn to others to get feedback, test jokes, and use the brainpower around them to punch up their work. I recommended a process for doing this in the most effective way in great detail in the second book in this series, *How to Write Funnier*.

In this book, that process is turbocharged. No longer will you simply be asking a group of peers to review your work and provide an opinion. Now you'll be incorporating their brainpower on an entirely different level. You're going to build a writers' room.

You're going to harness the one thing that created this revolution in comedy: swarms of people. You're going to infuse your own work with more brainpower, which will exponentially improve it. You're going to target your work like a laser and make it soar to the top of the heap, buoyed by a dedicated team of writers that's greater than the sum of its parts.

The best comedy of the last 50 years is the result of group efforts: *Monty Python's Flying Circus*, the seminal comedy sketch show that's inspired generations of comedy; *Saturday Night Live*, the longest running sketch show in TV history; *The Simpsons*, often named the best TV series of all time; *The Onion*, lauded as the most consistently funny humor publication in the world. All have won Peabody Awards. All have spawned writers and performers who have gone on to meteoric success. All are comedy institutions known for top-notch quality, prolific work, and spectacular writers' rooms.

FUNNIEST-WRITING TIP #1: CROWDSOURCE

*Corporations and online aggregators aren't the only ones who can crowdsource. Comedy writers can do so too. Working alone limits you as a comedy writer. If you have a comedy project, tell people about it and get them involved. If you're a stand-up, you already crowdsource when you test material in front of an audience. Consider working with someone to write material with you. If your comedy is public, people may approach you and ask to be involved. If they don't, solicit them. Reach out to people who share your sensibility on social media. Ask people in your feedback group, your circle of comedy friends, or anywhere else. The amount of their contribution can range from offering a few notes to participating in a full partnership. Offer to help them in return. However you arrange it, take advantage of the people power around you.*

Comedy writing may seem lonely, but it's the opposite. It requires a group no less than comedy performance does. Stand-up comics workshop and finalize their material using audience feedback the same way prose and sketch writers use writers' rooms. Even the amateurs on Twitter need likes and shares from other people to validate their best jokes. If no one is there to laugh at a piece of comedy, it can scarcely be called comedy.

So what's the secret to leveraging people power to make a writers' room? How do you utilize a writers' room to make your writing the best it can be? How do you find talented writers to be in your writers' room? How do you manage them and run meetings? How do you hold them together? How do you get them to work with you to make your writing far better than you can on your own? The answers are here.

We're all limited by our own inherent ability, not only our ability to write funny things, but our ability to work well with others. Most writing groups, comedy troupes, and writers' rooms fail. They rarely produce material that's better than the sum of their parts. More often they produce watered-down material, or worse, no material. Like rock bands, they fight and disagree until things get bitter, and then they break up with nothing to show for their efforts.

The first two books in this series focused on making you the best comedy writer you can be. This book focuses on joining forces with other great comedy writers who share your comedic vision, forming a comedy group, and inspiring that group to be the best group it can be, which will make you unstoppable.

The multitudes of amateur comedy writers that are driving this revolution will be your farm team. You'll select your writers from among their ranks. And it's these fellow comedy writers who are the secret to making your writing the funniest.

CHAPTER 1 ACTION STEP

*Read, re-read, or review any notes you have on the first two books in this series,* How to Write Funny *and* How to Write Funnier, *and do the action steps in each.*

## 2

# READY, FIRE, AIM

In almost all cases, there's one big bad thing that stops comedy writers from producing comedy prolifically. The same big bad thing stops them from putting together a team of writers to help them make their comedy the funniest it can be.

Before I lay out the process for managing a group of writers that churns out the funniest possible comedy, I need to address this one big bad thing and help you eliminate it.

In business, there's a famous saying (which oddly originated from Voltaire): "The perfect is the enemy of the good." The saying is famous because Voltaire, as well as most business and entrepreneurial experts, realized that the number-one problem facing new business people is the same problem facing almost all of us (and most certainly comedy writers) when it comes to pulling the trigger on a new endeavor: so many of us are perfectionists, especially (and counterintuitively) when we're unskilled beginners. And it's crippling us.

When you start doing anything in life, you won't do it well. It takes practice to get good at anything. Were you a great swimmer the first time you went into the water? Were you good at talking the first time you opened your mouth? Being a perfectionist in the beginning comes from a place of insecurity. You don't want to embarrass yourself by falling flat on your face. But just like when you learned to walk, you have to fall on your face—a lot—or you'll never learn.

Beginning comedy writers withhold material until they think it's perfect. When corralling a group of people together to make your comedy funnier, you're likely to do the same thing. You'll wait until the group is perfect. You'll wait until the proposal is perfect. You'll wait until anything and everything is perfect before you start.

---

FUNNIEST-WRITING TIP #2: START GOOD, NOT PERFECT

*One of the biggest weaknesses that afflicts creative people is perfectionism. In comedy and entertainment especially, creative people often feel hesitant to pull the trigger on a project, a joke, or a performance until it's what they consider "perfect." They'll spend a lot of time and money to make their comedy "perfect," not realizing they'd be better off making it "good enough" and then moving forward. Every work of comedy is an experiment to see if it will work. The quest for perfection is an illusion. The best policy is to bootstrap your efforts; start with whatever means you're able, and then learn as you go. You'll get better faster by proceeding with a "Start good, not perfect" attitude than you will with a "No, it has to be perfect" attitude.*

---

Don't aim first and then fire; fire first, learn a good lesson from how badly you missed, and then aim. Produce as much material as you can. Learn as much as you can from failing. (Failure, after all, is the best teacher.) Make your comedy as good as you can and put in front of audiences—immediately. Don't obsess about making it "perfect." The more you produce and distribute, and the faster you do it, the sooner you'll get good. And once you're good, you'll have an easier time attracting great team members. And then—and only then—will you even have a prayer of producing something "perfect." So be patient. Perfection, or something like it, will only come after a lot of imperfection. Get used to it.

By doing the best work you can when you start, regardless of how awful that work is, you set a powerful force in motion. You may think you're just pouring out bad work, but if you love doing comedy and you continue to do it, if you're open to feedback, and if you adjust what you're doing based on feedback, that's what pursuing comedy with passion looks like. And passion—especially a passion for improving yourself and succeeding at something difficult—is an attractive quality. Passion like this creates a force of gravity that draws like-minded people to you.

People starting out in comedy understand that they're expected to work for free to pay their dues. That's just the nature of the business. But you're not the only one working for free. Everybody else is too. In fact, everybody's working for less than free. They're likely spending a lot of money to do comedy (putting up a website, producing videos, buying books, and taking classes). When people at the same nascent stage in their comedy come together, each individual's comedy can be bolstered by the others.

# HOW TO FIND PEOPLE

Set your sights low. If you're just starting out, Patton Oswalt is not going to approach you about being a part of your team. And that's okay. Be patient with others and with yourself, start where you are, and plan to improve as you grow.

The type of people you're looking for are hardworking, ambitious, passionate about their own comedy, have a high EQ (Emotional Intelligence quotient), and are funny.

Try people out. If they don't jive with you, replace them with others.

Finding people is the easy part. The chapters that follow will cover the hard part: managing people.

# WHERE TO FIND PEOPLE

Start by looking at the people in your comedy circle and in your feedback group.

To expand your search, follow people you like on social media, people whose comedy style matches yours. Engage with them. DM them if they follow you back. Put out feelers. Let them know what you're working on and tell them you want them to be involved.

If your comedy is stand-up, tell them you want them to review your jokes and be your test audience. If you write sketch or prose, tell them you want to review their work if they'll review yours. Start building new comedy relationships.

If you have people locally you can meet with to discuss ideas and try out jokes, all the better. Start doing it and meet regularly. Don't wait to read this whole book before you start.

# HOW TO CONVINCE PEOPLE TO WORK WITH YOU

This is easier than you think. I've already given you the best re-cruiting tool: your own passionate and prolific comedy. This force of gravity may even inspire others to ask to join your efforts without your having to ask them. But when you ask, some people will agree to work with you.

Reciprocate. If they're also ambitious comedy creators, offer to be on their team. The more comedy you do, the better you're going to get at it. Operating as a leader of one group and a rank member of another will build tremendous team-building skills that will make you better at both.

Don't promise anything except the opportunity to produce comedy at first. Tips for structuring a writers' room that makes money is covered in chapters 9 and 10.

In the next chapters, you'll find insights into how to manage your team. The tips and guidance that follow will be far more resonant once you've formed a group and started working with them regularly.

Learn all you can by starting your own writing team now, and then improve your group and implement ideas you find in this book over time.

CHAPTER 2 ACTION STEPS

*1. Do your best work and produce a lot of it.*

*2. Begin following people on social media whose comedy you like, and whose style matches yours.*

*3. Reach out to these people as well as people in your feedback group, and invite them to be in your writers' room, virtual or physical.*

3

# CHIMPS

Chimps congregate in tightly knit groups called "communities," which are as large as 100 individuals. Within these communities, chimps form smaller subgroups, which vary in size and often break up. Males are in charge, and they lord over females despite the fact that females far outnumber males in most communities.

Imagine a small subgroup of chimps. A strong, healthy 20-year-old male is the alpha of the subgroup. We'll call him Alfred. Alfred and his small band of six chimps, some immature males and some females, are traipsing through the Congo in search of mangoes. One of the members of the group found one the other day, and the others fought over it so violently that Alfred had to break them up. They want more, so they're on another hunt.

Two of the chimps in the group form an alliance and stay within a few feet of each other to cover more ground. When they find a mango tree that has four or five good mangoes on it, they try to stay quiet and keep their discovery secret from Alfred in order to eat all the mangoes themselves. Alfred discovers them because one of the females loyal to him yelps an alert. Alfred chases the two young chimps away and takes the remaining mangoes for himself and his females.

One of the chimps passes a beehive and considers himself lucky for the instant snack, but he's not careful enough and suffers a few stings. He senses that the bees are going to swarm, so he runs. Some of the chimps laugh at his misfortune, while others try to console and comfort him.

One of the younger males backed by two others taunts Alfred, yanking the fur on his shoulder and then running away. Alfred bats at him but the young upstart sneaks back, half-heartedly picking a fight with him, imagining that without Alfred in charge, there might be more mangoes for him and his friends. When Alfred beats his chest and makes himself appear larger and acts like he's going to run after him, the young male bows, "play pants," and bares his teeth in a submissive gesture that looks a lot like human laughter.

Some females in the group leave the hunt and find sanctuary in another group with less tumult and a more magnanimous alpha. A couple of the males follow. With diminished confidence in the alpha, the rest of the group dissolves, having never found a bounty of mangoes.

Does any of this sound like your sketch troupe?

We all know humans and chimps share 98.8 percent of their DNA. Nowhere is this more evident than in a comedy writers' room.

When comedy people form groups, there's an alpha male (almost always a male), there's competition, there's symbolic grooming and the throwing of feces. Creating better comedy is the last thing on our minds. What's on our minds is, "Where do I fit in?" "Who's out to get me?" "Who's slighting whom?" And "Who should be in charge?"

Just like chimp groups, most comedy groups fall apart. People can't agree, so they squabble and scream. The end result is that the comedy they produce isn't funny.

On the plus side, comedy writers have 1.2 percent DNA that's uniquely human. And that sliver of difference (manifested partly in the uniquely human part of our brain, the frontal cortex) is enough to give us self-awareness beyond that of our primate cousins. We can temper our behavior when we know it will harm the group, and we can adopt new behavior when we believe it will lead to a greater, long-term good. Chimps aren't very good at these things. (Many humans aren't either, but I'm going to encourage you to try.) The ability to rise above our primate instincts is the best hope most comedy writers have to produce great work in a writers' room, yet most of us never think to take advantage of it, and it's why most comedy is mediocre.

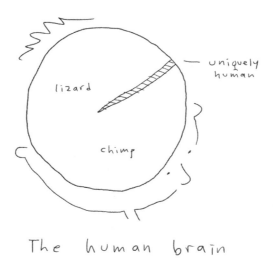

The human brain

Our chimpanzee instincts are incredibly powerful. They're a constant threat to our emotional stability. We can all agree intellectually that we're better off ignoring them and behaving like civilized humans, but this is far more easily said than done.

Managing a group of people is one of those skills that everyone thinks they're good at, but in reality any natural talent they think they have is probably no more than chimp instincts, which are unreliable at best. In fact, managing a group of people well is one of the most difficult skills to learn. It takes a high EQ, it takes pushing your ego aside and doing what's best for the group instead of yourself, and it takes focusing on long-term success, resisting instant gratification, and practicing.

Professional leaders and managers go to school for this stuff. They get business school degrees in business management. They get expensive leadership training. Yet even fancy business leaders who get this expensive education still act like chimps. No school, no matter how expensive, is going to erase 98.8 percent of someone's DNA. Some of these leaders with MBAs will become petty bosses who hoard credit, stoke dissent, and rule like chimpanzee alphas. Managing a group, no matter the size, is not a skill most people pick up naturally.

There are a number of good books you can get to dive deeper into this subject. Some good ones:

*The Effective Executive: The Definitive Guide to Getting the Right Things Done* by Peter Drucker
*How to Win Friends and Influence People* by Dale Carnegie
*The 5 Levels of Leadership* by John C. Maxwell

Comedy teams have a reputation for being especially difficult to manage. They're iconoclastic. They're creative thinkers. They don't like authority. They don't like structure. Many people compare leading comedy people to herding cats.

In lieu of a long and costly MBA or a ream of business books, there are shortcuts for managing a comedy group to rein them in and compel them to create exponentially funnier comedy than they could ever hope to create on their own. This book lays out the best practices, but it will take eternal vigilance to live up to them. Your instincts and emotions will be pulling you constantly and powerfully in the wrong direction.

The crux of the challenge is to think with the 1.2 percent of your brain, and ignore the 98.8 percent.

In addition to the tiny part of our brains that's uniquely human, and the vast majority that's chimp, there's a good portion of the whole that's reptilian. Yes, we share 98.8 percent of our brains with chimps, but we also share about 65 percent of our brains with prehistoric reptiles. Our ancient ancestors, before becoming mammals, were sea creatures and other proto-lizards. This means we have a base brain that compels us to survive, reproduce, and hunt, just like a lizard's brain. On top of that we have the more evolved, nuanced needs of a mammal: social cohesion, emotional connection, and love. Only in a tiny sliver of our brains do we have human-level abstract reasoning and intelligence.

These older parts of our brains were selected by evolution and adapted perfectly to survive in the primitive environments where they thrived. In a modern writers' room, they aren't much use.

Being a human, especially one trying to lead a team of comedy writers, is like trying to ride a chimp that's riding a dinosaur.

---

FUNNIEST-WRITING TIP #3: LEAVE YOUR EGO AT THE DOOR

*In a writers' room, there are myriad temptations to blow off steam, get defensive, sass back, or otherwise let your ego get the best of you. You need to avoid any behavior motivated by an urge to protect your ego, and you need to conduct yourself like a professional. It's not easy to maintain your composure in a writers' room; the context and the energy in that room encourages unrestrained thinking, passionate expression, and vulnerability. It takes discipline to keep a lid on every emotion in such an atmosphere. But it's essential. When egos flare in a writers' room, it becomes a toxic, dark place, like a black hole from which no comedy can escape.*

---

We are a mess of emotions and drives that we barely understand, and these awful forces come to play when we're under stress, in a group, and trying to produce comedy. Avoiding getting snared in the traps laid by the primitive parts of our brains takes some keen stealth. Our drives are part of us, and we can't just flip a switch and turn them off.

Or can we?

CHAPTER 3 ACTION STEP

*Hold a meeting with your new writing group, either virtual or actual, and settle on a comedy project to pursue. After the meeting, make notes about how you think the meeting went. You'll compare these notes to the details you'll find later in this book. For now, it's important to start, and then learn by doing.*

# 4

# MYTH VS. REALITY

Several jaded and cynical writers laze around in a messy writers' room that looks like a glorified college dorm lounge. One's feet are crossed on top of his desk, and he's bouncing a ball off the wall, two are arm-wrestling, and another is trying to throw a crumpled-up piece of paper into a trash can across the room. The head writer is flipping through papers, reading jokes.

An eager young writer sits up in the writers' room all of a sudden.

"Hey everybody, I've got a great idea!"

They all stop what they're doing and look.

"Yeah? Whad'ya got?" one asks.

"It's about a comedy writer who can't think of an idea."

Some of the writers sit up.

"Okay, I'm intrigued," the one bouncing the ball says.

"I can relate to this one!" an arm-wrestler says.

"He's sitting in the writers' room," the young writer says, "and he has no idea, so he pitches an idea that's literally *no idea*."

"So, he doesn't pitch?" the head writer asks.

"No, he pitches a non-idea. It's like the John Cage piece. The comedy version of his four minutes of silence!"

A couple of the writers who get the obscure reference chuckle knowingly.

The head writer thinks a minute, then says, "Yeah, okay, I get it. It's the absence of comedy that makes it funny."

"Exactly!"

A writer offers some additional beats: "One writer nods. Another one points. But it's all silent." Laughter peppers the room.

"Then someone starts taking notes on the idea," another writer jokes. This gets the whole room laughing.

Someone offers, "The head writer says, 'it's too long,' and the writer says, 'don't worry, the non-laughs will pad it out.'"

More laughs.

The head writer points to a junior writer and says, "Start typing this out. This is good." The junior writer starts typing.

Someone else proposes, "It becomes like Jack Benny's longest laugh in radio history—but it's the longest period of *no* laughter ever."

Other riffs fly:

"He acts it out by just sitting there, not doing anything."

"The head writer points to one of them randomly—someone not doing or saying anything—and says, 'oh yeah, I like that—that's really good!'"

"The sketch wins an Emmy and no one claps at the award ceremony and the writer accepting the Emmy doesn't say anything."

"They spin it off into an animated series."

Now the room is consumed with uncontrollable laughter.

Eventually they settle down. They can't believe how hard they laughed! The head writer motions for everyone to stop riffing. "Okay, read back what we got."

The junior writer reads through the whole sketch and the writers love it.

"Alright," the head writer says, "it's settled—we've nailed the opening sketch for tonight's show!"

You've seen this scenario if you've ever watched *The Dick Van Dyke Show*, heard stories of the *Your Show of Shows* writers' room, or seen just about any entertainment-industry depiction of a comedy writers' room.

This fanciful room is bursting with positive energy. Writers are having fun, cracking each other up with every utterance, and creating comedy gold on the first try, purely through lightning-bolt-style inspiration without even trying.

The writers' room

myth                              reality

The idea of a writers' room like this is largely why a people unconnected with comedy often harbor secret fantasies of working on a TV comedy show. It would be so much fun to be in those meetings!

The writers work together, riffing on each others' ideas, and their riffs are brilliant, flowing naturally from the core idea. The act of riffing itself is a magical way that funny material gets created. Their jokes flow easily, with the whole room performing like a seasoned jazz band, no one striking a discordant note. Each joke is better than the last, and builds the sketch to a hilarious finish.

This writers' room scenario might happen once in a rare while, but almost never. It's akin to a hole-in-one in golf. Another way to understand how unlikely it is, is to compare it to the way chess games are depicted on TV shows and movies without fail: player one makes a surprising move and says "check." Then player two makes an even more surprising move and says, "checkmate." Then the game is over. A game of chess almost never ends this way in real life, but the myth is relentless in popular culture.

If you ran your writers' room like in this scenario, you'd be almost guaranteed of never producing good comedy. In fact, it's a recipe for bad comedy. It's also a recipe for bruised egos, Machiavellian maneuvers, infighting, and screaming matches. Real writers in a real writers' room are almost never having fun. They're at work. This is their job.

Magic sometimes happens in a writers' room. And sometimes fun happens too. But more often than not, it happens when the writers are not actually writing. It happens when they're just palling around before a meeting or during their lunch break. It's rare that the funny things writers say in those moments are suitable for actual comedy material meant for an audience. A great sketch, scene, or idea is rarely going to spring from this kind of off-the-cuff joking around. To create usable comedy, writers are more likely to be staring into a computer screen, stone-faced, trying hard to think of funny things to write about.

When writers riff on a random idea that someone thinks up in a meeting, more often than not, the concept itself is flawed. It's a "room joke," only understandable to the writers in the room (like the meta-joke concocted by the writers above). An uninitiated audience has little hope of understanding it, let alone appreciating it. But most writers get caught up in the excitement of the riffing. They don't recognize the inaccessible joke for what it is, and therefore the final result is worthless.

Or—this happens constantly—the concept is actually good, but the writers riff the wrong take, veering into territory that yields increasingly unusable material.

Once riffing gets started, the energy in a writers' room is like a moving train that gets harder to stop with every new joke that's riffed. Anyone who recognizes the futility of the effort and expends precious leadership capital to end it is branded a buzzkill, or worse, a creativity killer.

What is a real writers' room like? Here are the five most common:

### The despotic writers' room

Because our hunter-gatherer instinct and our chimp and reptilian

DNA can't be escaped, humans tend to end up with writers' rooms run by despots, strong-willed authoritarian head writers or editors who rule by fiat. Though perhaps useful for survival to our ancestors on the African savannah, these despots make for less-than-ideal head writers, producers, or editors. It's not the quality of the work that rules the day in these rooms, it's the ego of the alpha.

Writers' rooms like this are cesspools of conflict. Everyone worries more about what the alpha will like than what's genuinely funny. Everyone wants to be in the alpha's good favor. Everyone fears the alpha's wrath.

Sometimes this conflict is overt, with a lot of screaming and fighting. Other times it's subtle, like in the back-stabbing, boot-licking courts of Medieval Europe. Petty and power-hungry connivers jockey for position within the ranks of the writing staff. Writers act chummily and cooperatively on the surface, but are deeply competitive underneath, happy to sacrifice a fellow writer's esteem in order to achieve a perceived advancement, no matter how small.

### The fear-based writers' room

On the African savannah, when lives were on the line, fear may have been a more effective tool for social cohesion than compassion or understanding. But when a writers' room is ruled by fear (fear of the alpha's wrath, fear of being fired, or fear or being ridiculed for a bad joke), material is doomed to be weak because no one will dare speak honestly or take any creative risk.

A fear-based writers' room often goes hand-in-hand with a despotic one.

### The loner-alpha writers' room

Another type of writers' room is also run by an alpha, but the alpha doesn't rule by an iron fist. Instead the alpha is weak and avoids conflict. Comedy creation in this kind of room is a one-person show. This alpha is someone who enjoys doing all the work, prefers to work alone, and employs a team only reluctantly. This alpha is often antisocial or uniquely wedded to the vision of the project, skeptical that anyone else can produce work in the proper voice or of the proper quality. These alphas will lock themselves in their one-person office and generally shut everyone else out.

### The "just a job" writers' room

In some writers' rooms, the writers aren't fueled by passion or a desire to do good work, but rather a paycheck. Writing is their day job. Professional union writers' rooms are prone to this syndrome. Everyone's being paid well, they often have job security (such as it is, with some surviving only on 13-week contracts), and their top priority is not creating amazing comedy, it's preserving their standard of living.

Writers' rooms like this are sometimes competently run. At least they're not fear-based tyrannies. The "just a job" writers' room feels like a pleasant enough workplace where everyone is happy to show up in the morning, but they check out at the end of the work day. They aren't necessarily devoted to the project, nor do they have the drive to keep working after the whistle blows. Professionals who write like this produce competent (though not groundbreaking or hilarious), formulaic comedy. This type of room rarely produces the funniest comedy—the kind that becomes a cultural touchstone.

---

FUNNIEST-WRITING TIP #4: BUILD A CULTURE

*Whether you realize you're doing it or not, you're building a culture when you're putting together a group of writers to collaborate on a project. You have a tremendous amount of power in any writers' room. Your behavior in the writers' room contributes to the culture of the room, and the culture determines how much fun the other writers are having, how much they'll produce, how fulfilling the work is, and how funny the output is. Your behavior in a writers' room, good or bad, will rub off on everyone else. If you're on your best behavior, you'll raise the stakes for the entire endeavor.*

---

### The committee-run writers' room

Most amateur group-written comedy isn't very good. The problem can often be traced to the way their meeting is run: by committee. Running a room by committee is even worse than running it by fiat. It all but guarantees that the comedy produced will be bland. When everyone has to come to a consensus that something is funny, this usually means no one is particularly excited about it. In this type of writers' room, it goes against the group culture to point out when something's not funny. Such a comment would be a serious faux pas in a committee-run writers' room, and possibly grounds for dismissal.

"Let me guess—comedy writer"

Writers' rooms can be a mix of these five, and even individual writers can embody the culture of each of these types of writers' rooms and bring that with them when they leave one writers' room and join another.

Here are some qualities common to almost every writers' room:

• They suffer a high turnover rate, which prevents the group from ever developing the bonds or the room culture that cause a unique group voice to develop.

• They demand absurdly long hours, especially on TV shows. Writers are often expected to work 12-hour days. When they're in the Writer's Guild, they get mandated breaks to prevent burnout, but any writer can tell you that those breaks are barely adequate. Writers are often exhausted, which makes it challenging to show up with the passion necessary to make their work great.

• They produce a lot of material that's not funny, including the final, approved material. Funny material is often being written, but it's unrecognized because the alpha didn't think of it or believes it doesn't align with the group voice. Hard work is going to waste because the team isn't using the best practices of a writers' room.

• They're Machiavellian, even the committee-run rooms. Without structures in place to correct for the chimp-brain tendency to compete for significance within a group, the work of the funniest writer doesn't rise to the top. Instead, the work of most persuasive writer does.

• They're dreary places, like any workplace, that writers can't wait to leave.

• They're high-stress, busy places where writers are always hard at work chasing deadlines.

In the next chapter and beyond, we'll look at what an ideal writers' room looks like, and how to set it up and manage it so it's a productive, fun place where writers feel like they're on the same mission, all working joyously toward the greater good of coming up with the funniest possible writing.

## CHAPTER 4 ACTION STEP

*Take a hard look at your writers' room. Does it look like any of the writers' rooms described in this chapter?*

# 5

# WHO ARE THESE PEOPLE?

Every writers' room is populated by the same nine people. Without fail, you'll see some combination of these nine possible meeting-attendee archetypes at every gathering of comedy writers. They fill predictable though unofficial roles, some helpful, others less so. But all can contribute to a successful writers' room.

Each of these nine team members has a part to play in crafting comedy. Each one can be drawn out to bolster and support the best comedy ideas of the others through competent management of the team and the protocol employed. (See chapters 6, 7, 9, and 12 for details.)

These roles are not always straightforward. A writer in a group can embody more than one role. The roles often behave like masks, put on and taken off by different team members in different situations. It's a mistake to assume that anyone is permanently in one state or another. In the end, you can work with each of these roles to inspire them to contribute to a comedy-writing process that generates the funniest material.

Here's a list of these nine roles, what function they serve, and how to work with them:

**The Leader**

The Leader runs the meeting. Leaders are alphas. In an alpha-run meeting, the Leader can take one of four forms:

• The Tyrant

Some Leaders are Tyrants who control all aspects of the work. The Leader is the one person everyone is working to please. When you're a lowly member of this kind of group, pleasing the ultimate comedy audience is less important than pleasing the Leader during the meeting. Tyrants often lead by fear, creating a stressful environment where writers are afraid of being ridiculed, called out, yelled at, or fired.

• The Loner-Alpha

Some Leaders are Loner-Alphas, who close themselves off to the other writers on the team to work alone, only sometimes taking the staff's suggestions and possibly incorporating them into the shared work, but only when they see fit. The Loner-alpha doesn't communicate well to the underlings, and often hides in a secluded office.

• The Bureaucrat

The Bureaucrat is nominally in charge, but low on charisma. The Bureaucrat values the process, and tends toward committee-run meetings. The Bureaucrat wants to do the best job possible and will always be open to new ways of doing things.

• The Best Boss

The Best Boss is a Leader who understands what motivates people on a team and strives to give it to them. The Best Boss is likable and agreeable, and is also generally inspiring when it comes to the work. They're the most pleasant kind of Leader to work with, of course, but the Best Boss doesn't necessarily lead to the best comedy.

The Leader is typically the most active person in the writers' room. They may be a head writer, producer, or editor. Either self-appointed, appointed by a boss, or appointed by group vote, the Leader takes on the ultimate responsibility of delivering the final comedy material, either by doing it themselves or delegating to others with varying degrees of supervision. There's only one way to deal with any kind of Leader to get the best comedy, and that is to take on the role of the Helper (below). (See Chapters 6, 7, and 12 for more on the Leader.)

## The Helper

Another of the nine people in the writers' room is the Helper. The Helper is the second-most valuable member of the team, next to the Leader. The Helper assists the Leader in any way needed. They volunteer to take on any delegated tasks, help run meetings, or handle organizational tasks. In a dysfunctional writers' room, the Helper may be misidentified as a toady, but in a properly run writers' room, the Helper assists without threatening the Leader's position. The same is true in a dysfunctional meeting, though only at first. (Soon enough, in a dysfunctional meeting, the Helper is actively plotting to take over the Leader's position.) A secure Leader will never be threatened by a good Helper. They are, at their best, a loyal second-in-command. Every effective Leader is made better by a good Helper.

The Helper is often resented by other team members because they're seen as a kiss-ass, and often don't do a lot of comedy writing; they may be more interested in assisting the Leader administratively. Regardless, allow the Helper to help in any way that's needed. Encourage them to create more comedy if they're not creating much. Or, conversely, if they're too focused on writing comedy, urge them to be more of an administrative help if that's needed. They'll work hard, aim to please, and likely become a great contributor on all fronts, even if they begin as someone without much promise. In comedy, hard work and practice are everything. (See Chapter 8 for more on the Helper.)

## The Loner

Another member of the writers' room is the Loner. The Loner shouldn't be confused with the Loner-Alpha Leader. This kind of Loner is a rank-and-file team member who doesn't talk much in the group. They prefer to keep to themselves and keep their mouth shut. Some Loners are merely shy. Others may have deeper social anxiety (one of the many emotional challenges the field of comedy is famous for). While a shortsighted Leader might dismiss a Loner as someone who's not gelling with the team, the wise Leader takes the opportunity to recognize and appreciate the Loner's quiet contributions and will encourage them to participate more. The Loner is often one of the most competent and productive members of a writing team.

The 9 comedy writers

**The Disagreer**

In contrast with the Helper, the Disagreer is always ready to play devil's advocate. They see the incongruity in situations, pointing out the minority opinion, regardless of whether anyone else is expressing it. Sometimes they don't necessarily hold the opinion in question; they just feel the need to express it. They're the most skeptical member of the team about not only the comedy material at hand, but also operational matters. The Disagreer will get into arguments with the Leader or anyone else who will engage with them, believing that dissenting opinion is valuable and leads to greater understanding. A Disagreer's opinion does in fact lead to greater understanding for them, because finding the differences in things is how they make sense of the world. But a lot of people are uncomfortable with the Disagreer. They see a Disagreer as someone who's insubordinate or unnecessarily combative.

A weak Leader can't easily abide a Disagreer. Some Leaders may even consider firing a Disagreer for not playing along. But a secure Leader will recognize that the Disagreer often voices the most valuable opinion in the room. They're someone who can stave off committee thinking. They're someone who, wittingly or not, keeps everyone honest about what material is really working, or what part of the process could be improved.

The Disagreer needs to be heard, even when their counterpoint seems annoying. If everyone else loves a comedy concept, the Disagreer may be the lone holdout who recognizes it as bad, and we always need to listen to the "no" vote. Think very carefully about whether the Disagreer might be more in tune with the potential audience than everyone else in the room. Groupthink can take over a writers' room easily, blinding everyone to how audiences will ultimately perceive their work, The Disagreer is a constant reminder that skepticism is always the best policy.

### The Workhorse

A lot of writers are only capable of a limited number of good writing hours in a day due to their energy level or mental capacity. A Workhorse, on the other hand, can write circles around other writers. They work harder than anyone else, sometimes as a matter of pride, sometimes just to satisfy their natural compulsion to work. Other times, they're overtly or subliminally driven to compete with other writers on the team. In any case, the Workhorse can always be trusted to deliver a good volume of material and get a lot of things done.

Though a godsend to any team, a Workhorse often needs mandated time off. It's easy for a Leader to rely on a Workhorse and overwork them to the point of burnout. They love working so much, they'll never protest. But you don't want to see a Workhorse crack. There's a reason they work so hard. They may be compensating for deep emotional pain by writing all the time. Treat their work with the respect it deserves. Help them manage their compulsion to write with some well-deserved breaks. Encouraging them to step away occasionally not only keeps them producing at their maximum capacity but also keeps them satisfied.

**The Drag**

In contrast with the Workhorse is the Drag. The Drag doesn't get much done, and what they do get done is often the result of a lot of nagging from the Leader or Helper. They do the minimum amount of writing to get by, if that. Often, they're the most vocal member of the group. While the Drag may seem like dead weight to some, a smart Leader recognizes that someone who's more vocal in the room as opposed to productive on the page is providing a worthwhile service.

The Drag may need a talking-to on occasion to step up, but remember to separate their work ethic from the comedy value they bring to the team. If their comedy is good, respect that. You'll never get as much comedy from them as you'll get from a Workhorse, but they can be equally valuable. Appreciating what work you do get from the Drag, and gently (perhaps consistently) urging them to produce more is a small price to pay to keep their brain power involved in the group.

**The Intellectual**

The Intellectual takes comedy seriously and can discuss comedy theory endlessly. This can be valuable at times, but can also be a distraction. The Intellectual can deconstruct why jokes work or don't work, which is an important voice to have in a group. They can also bog down a brainstorming or riffing session by merely talking *about* the joke concepts being tossed around instead of providing an opinion or proposing new joke ideas.

The Intellectual can sometimes derail conversations or riffing. A little nudging to keep them on target is often all it takes to redirect their intellectual prowess to the generation of comedy.

**The Joker**

In contrast with the Intellectual, the Joker doesn't take anything seriously. In order to produce comedy competently and on deadline, sometimes serious discussions have to take place, but the Joker is always there to lighten the mood and mock everything. Rank-and-file team members typically love and value the Joker. Some Leaders, on the other hand (burdened with the stress of running the meeting and producing the product), become annoyed with the Joker. But if the Joker's comedy energy can be channeled into the actual material, and the riffing that needs to happen with all ideas, they can be among the most productive contributors. The Joker should be celebrated. If they veer too far from the task of producing usable comedy, a little urging now and then to direct their comedy energy to the work at hand will never be resented.

FUNNIEST-WRITING TIP #5: TRUST THE "NO" VOTE

*When discussing comedy in a group, one writer will sometimes dislike a concept that the rest of the group loves. While it would be easy to dismiss the lone dissenting opinion, a smart writers' room listens carefully and respectfully to the "no" vote before barreling ahead and presenting the concept to an audience. That lone dissenting opinion is likely the closest thing you have to an end-audience avatar. Your audience will always be less excited about your comedy creations than you are. If you're performing on stage and using the crowd's reaction to test your jokes, you won't learn about this dissenting opinion during the performance. You'll hear about it afterwards. If a joke killed during the show but a small minority tell you how unfunny it was after the show, you need to listen to that opinion. It could be the opinion of a tastemaker cautioning you against going too low-brow. Or it could be someone warning you about a looming political backlash should you adopt the joke as a regular part of your set.*

### The Glue

The Glue is the person who keeps everyone together. They rally the team to stay united and positive when things seem dire. If the writers' room is having trouble making something funny, the Glue will be there with a pep talk, to cheerlead the group and remind everyone what great things they can achieve. The Leader is often the Glue, but not always. The Glue can be a rank-and-file team member. A smart Leader will recognize the Glue for the value they bring, creating camaraderie and a positive attitude in the writers' room. The Glue should be appreciated and welcomed openly for the supportive role they play.

As you'll see in Chapter 9, a writers' room has to be run the right way to get the best results. Wherever there are humans, there's drama. But knowing who's on your team and how to treat them—even if you're not the Leader—will set you up with a writers' room that has minimal drama and maximum comedy output. You'll enjoy a meeting where each individual is not subliminally trying to survive in the jungle, but rather melding minds, committed to the collective creation of the funniest possible comedy.

CHAPTER 5 ACTION STEP

*Identify yourself and the other people in your new writing team and use the guidance in this chapter to improve the way you interact with each type of team member during meetings.*

# 6

# TAKING THE REINS

By now you've identified what role you typically play in the writers' room. But what role is best for you? It might not be the one you're currently playing.

If you've been appointed head writer or editor and been charged with running a writers' room, you should be the Leader. If it's your project and you corralled all the writers to be on the team, you should be the Leader. If you're in a committee-run group that has no Leader, you should be the Leader. If there's a nominal Leader but that Leader is weak and there's a leadership vacuum, you should be the Leader.

In any other scenario, if you identified yourself as any of the other types besides the Leader or the Helper in the previous chapter, or if you have no desire to be the Leader, you should strive to be the Helper.

The only situation in which you should be neither the Leader nor the Helper is when you're already the Leader but you've decided to delegate the leadership responsibilities to a trusted lieutenant so you can tackle bigger issues on the project beyond running the writers' room. But know that when you delegate such an important role, whomever you appoint may make some decisions you're not happy with. You need to encourage and support that person, and also stay in close contact with them to help them stay on voice. This happens when, for example, a TV show creator writes the pilot episode and runs the first few meetings, but then appoints a head writer to run the writers' meetings while the creator handles more producorial or executive duties.

Don't ever mutiny. There's a process for becoming the Leader that's fair and acceptable and that won't alienate people (see below). Aggressively vying for power is off-putting. Being the Helper, on the other hand, doesn't threaten anyone, and any writer at any level can and should be the Helper.

If you're in a committee-run group with no clear Leader, the process for becoming a Leader is to invite discussion of options for how to structure the group differently. Propose the idea of structuring the group according to the best practices outlined in this book. Then propose that the group discuss and vote on who should lead. If you've played your cards right and done everything in this book, you'll likely be elected the Leader.

If you're in a group that has a weak Leader or there's a leadership vacuum, or if the Leader isn't responsible, you can become the Leader by being an unflappably good Helper. Do this by politely volunteering to take some of the load off the Leader. Offer to run the meetings and take care of any responsibilities that the Leader wants to pass off to you. If the Leader is late and you show up on time, you can begin running the meeting. In time, the group will accept you as the Leader, even if you don't have an official leadership job title. Ask for a promotion after you've been doing this good work. Ask for a job title change when you feel you've earned it. But never complain if it's refused. Just continue to be the best Helper you can be (see chapter 8). If you continue to play nice, work hard, and live up to or exceed your responsibilities, the leadership reins will eventually fall to you. If they don't, or if you're feeling impatient, you can leave the writers' room and start your own. Many of the writers in the group will probably follow you. People follow a Leader.

If you're not the Leader, or if you're the Leader but you feel like your leadership is in jeopardy, one strategy to bolster your authority is to ally yourself with the person with the strongest natural leadership qualities in the group. There's usually one person in the group (they may be the Joker, the Loner, the Workhorse, or anyone) who's widely respected by the team and has effortless leadership qualities. They may be louder or more extroverted, or they may just be especially likable. This person may not be interested in being the Leader, or they may not be appointed the Leader. But you can ally yourself with that person. Deputize them as a Helper, delegate an important responsibility to them, or give them a job title. These moves put them in direct cooperation with you and will strengthen your leadership.

To illustrate this principle of allying with the strongest natural leader in the group, look no further than *Rise of the Planet of the Apes*. Caesar successfully took over the animal-control shelter from the previous alpha by allying himself with the imposing gorilla, whom all the other chimps feared and respected.

If you can unseat the Leader in a non-violent coup, that also works.

But unseating a Leader can be a messy process that's best avoided. Better to be patient and take a leadership position when you can naturally slide into it, not when you take it by force. Mutinous Leaders rarely hold onto leadership for long.

Once you're the Leader of the writers' room, you have the following responsibilities (in no particular order):

### Build consensus

Even if your writers' room is not a committee-run room, the idea of a committee or democracy is important to most writers. Every writer wants to know that they have a voice and that their voice is heard. So even though, as the Leader, you have the final say and final veto power over ideas, you don't want to be seen wielding that power capriciously. If you do, you'll be perceived as a Tyrant. But by asking everyone's opinion and making sure there's discussion of every idea before you make a decision, and by deferring to the collective judgment of the group when you have no reason to defy it, you'll be perceived as a fair and magnanimous Leader. On rare occasion you may need to break with the group one way or the other (to push an idea everyone hates or reject an idea everyone loves), but as long as you err on the side of building consensus most of the time, such extreme pushes will be tolerated if not outright accepted.

### Check your ego at the door

If you're the Leader, you can't champion your own ideas, even if you think they're hilarious. You need to trust the judgment of your team and leave your personal feelings aside. And this goes beyond comedy concepts. The Leader has to remain above the fray in all matters. If emotions get heated, which they often do in a writers' room, the Leader has to keep a cool head. It's the Leader's job to deescalate tension, not throw gasoline on it. This requires, at a minimum, tempering your own ego, and it's an undertaking that may take constant diligence.

### Encourage egoless behavior

Keeping ego in check doesn't stop with the Leader. The Leader has to encourage everyone on the team to check their egos at the door too. When ego seeps into discussion, the writers' room descends into chimp territory.

By keeping ego at bay, the room produces more good material.

**Make it clear that you're in charge**

If at any moment the Leader seems weak, inattentive, uninvolved, or uninspired, the other writers in the group will sense a leadership vacuum. If anyone tries to usurp the Leader in any way, the Leader needs to step in and subtly assert authority. This is best done silently and subliminally.

Taking on all of the responsibilities in this chapter (as well as embodying the qualities in the next chapter) will serve to make it clear that you're in charge.

---

FUNNIEST-WRITING TIP #6: USE CHIMP BEHAVIOR TO YOUR ADVANTAGE

*The overriding theme of this book so far is that we must rise above our chimp instincts, but because we're more than 98 percent chimp, some chimp instincts are useful. Chimp-like bonding and dominance cues can be used to subtly display leadership. People who stand up straight and fill the space around them (either with height, grand gestures, or just good posture) are people we subconsciously identify as Leaders. Patting someone (appropriately) on the back or shoulder is a display of dominance. Praising someone's good work and rewarding them in some way (with a compliment or even a gift) is a power move. You might use some of these tactics unknowingly, but they're nonetheless effective subliminal messages that should be in every Leader's toolbox when running a writers' room.*

---

**Hear every opinion**

The easiest way to weaken a group is for one member to feel unheard. Always make sure everyone expresses their views. If a writer or writers is quiet, draw them out and ask them what they think. When people know you hear them, they're more apt to trust you as a Leader.

**Praise publicly**

People on your team should always be praised for their hard work as

"This meeting is called to order."

well as any instances of success. For maximum benefit, praise deliberately as a public announcement, in front of the entire group, to make sure everyone is aware of the good work or good deed done. For major successes, praise is best dished out at the top of a meeting when you can introduce new business with deliberately celebratory words for a select member of the team. Praise is cheap and an extremely effective way to not only instill respect as a Leader but also to keep morale high. Even a small thing like singling out a writer by name and complimenting them for a passing joke during a riffing session goes a long way.

### Reprimand privately

Sometimes Leaders need to deal with a personnel problem. If someone on the team disparages someone else, fails to show up, turns in an assignment late, or the like, these actions have to be corrected, but never in front of others. Public humiliation is the least effective form of behavior modification. Positive reinforcement, on the other hand, almost always yields the behavior change you want. When recurring bad behavior has to be addressed, do it quietly, alone with the individual, and allow them to rise to the occasion with dignity once they're back among the group.

### Diffuse emotion

In addition to keeping ego out of the writers' room, it's important to keep destructive emotions out too. People on a project or at a job, thanks to our chimpanzee brains, tend to think of their co-workers as their tribe or extended family. But the smart Leader always keeps in mind that these people you're producing comedy with are not your family or your tribe. They're your co-workers, and you're together only to produce a comedy project, not to form familial bonds. Emotional bonds will develop naturally, of course; nothing can stop that—and loose ties can be helpful to bond a group—but the deeper the connection, the more the risk that emotional pain will interfere with sound comedy judgement. The Leader's job is to allow emotion as appropriate, but make sure it doesn't negatively impact the project.

The Leader has to play den mother, urging everyone in the writers' room to stay professional. Understanding and accepting emotional outbursts on occasion is important—they will happen—but a Leader needs to step in quickly to quell any outbursts and remind the entire group to stay focused on the comedy.

### Set the tone

The Leader determines the tone of the room. If the Leader is bouncy and energetic, the meetings will be fast-paced and fun. If the Leader is morose, the meeting will be a downer. If the Leader is serious and focused, the meetings will be efficient and productive. When you're the Leader, choose wisely and choose consciously what you want the tone of your writers' room to be.

### Put people at ease

A Leader should be approachable and easygoing, not tense and off-putting. Writers won't perform well if the tone of the writers' room is tense. When the Leader puts people at ease, the team is more comfortable sharing their ideas, taking risks, and working together.

### Be funny

If you're not a natural performer, or you don't think you're good on your feet, being funny as a Leader may seem like a tall order, but it's important in a comedy writers' room. A Leader doesn't necessarily need to be "on." In fact, that might be annoying to the other writers. But the

Leader has to be themselves, be relaxed, and try to cultivate a fun, self-deprecating, or sardonic attitude at least—anything to lighten the mood of the meeting and help put everyone at ease. (See chapter 15 for a look at how to be funny under pressure.)

### Focus on the quality of the work

The Leader has to remain focused above all on the quality of the work, always working to clear other feelings and challenges out of the way.

Being the Leader of a writers' room is a lot like being a stand-up comedian. A comedian goes on stage and has to bury all of their stage fright, anxiety, self-doubt, and fears in order to focus like a laser on delivering the highest quality performance and the funniest possible material. The Leader of a writers' room has to bury all the challenges of managing a group of people and then deliver the highest quality leadership in order to facilitate the funniest possible material.

### Have integrity

A Leader needs to be reliable, do what they say they're going to do, and follow through. Little gestures like making deadlines (even unofficial ones), being accountable, and being on time—carried out consistently—will work toward engendering the respect that a Leader needs in order to lead.

### Be inspiring

To be a Leader people will rally around and be excited to work with, make people feel like they're part of something important and special. This will inspire them by making them feel like they belong. This is an area where you can use chimp instincts to your advantage: while you don't want the emotional baggage of a tribe, you want the motivating team spirit of a tribe. (See chapter 7 for more tips on how to inspire your team.)

CHAPTER 6 ACTION STEPS

*1. If you're the Leader of your team, take on the responsibilities in this chapter. If you're not the Leader of your writing team, become a Helper.*

*2. If you've taken on the Helper role, ask the Leader to let you lead a meeting to practice taking on the responsibilities in this chapter without usurping the Leader's authority.*

# BEING BOSSY

Bob Hope was one of the first stand-up comedians who admitted he had writers. Even when he didn't have his popular radio show in the 1930s, he was the Leader of a (mostly) virtual writers' room comprised of short-term-contract joke writers similar to the staff of a late-night talk show today.

Comedians before him surely hired joke writers, but they preferred to keep that knowledge behind the scenes, so that audiences would think them capable of coming up with incredible one-liners off the top of their heads whenever they made public appearances. In the latter half of the twentieth century, audiences came to accept the idea that comedy performers did indeed hire writers. Johnny Carson's near-daily Metahumor often referred to his staff of writers. David Letterman went further, putting his writers in front of the camera.

Recently, the old stigma has returned. There's a point of pride among some comics today about working alone. Jerry Seinfeld is a famous example. Comics like this prefer to write all their own jokes because, they say, this is how they keep their comedy voice pure. But some comics still employ writers. Some admit it, some don't.

No matter what medium of comedy you're in—stand-up, animation, comic strips, you name it—you're well served by having a team of writers back you up if you want your writing to be the funniest it can possibly be. The most successful comedians know this. (Even Seinfeld employed writers for his TV show, of course.)

When you begin to build a team to work on comedy that's in your voice, or in the voice of whatever comedy project you're spearheading, you're the Leader. The Leader is the custodian of the comic voice, the one person who will decide if the material is funny, if it's in character, and if it's on voice.

But these aren't the only responsibilities of a Leader. Once you become a Leader of a team, you take on a bigger burden than just writing jokes. Now you're a boss, and you have to wrestle with all the chimp DNA that starts to come into play when you're thrust into a hierarchical group.

Your most important task as a Leader is to minimize the influence of your (and your group's) chimp DNA and maximize the laugh quotient of what you and your team produces. This chapter lays out the most important actions a Leader can take to achieve this ideal.

### A Leader has a vision

The single defining trait of a good Leader is vision. The Leader must have an articulated aspiration or mission in order to inspire a team. The vision doesn't have to be a placard on the wall with a mission statement on it. It can be communicated verbally or in writing. But it must be clear to everyone. In comedy, the vision usually entails putting forth a unique comedic voice, and making that voice as funny as possible. A Leader who pursues a vision passionately will not only attract team members, but will also likely have an easier time managing them. Most importantly, a team with a shared vision is more likely to appeal to audiences.

Even a Leader who has nothing else, who's timid and thoughtless—a bad Leader by any other measure—will have enough strength to lead if only they have a strong vision. Conversely, a strong Leader who excels at all aspects of good leadership, yet has no vision, will not last long.

The Leader is the final arbiter of the voice of the group. They have veto power over ideas, and ultimate decision-making power over which ideas get presented to audiences. In every practical way, the voice of the group is the voice of the Leader. The best Leaders let their voice be augmented and strengthened by their teams, becoming a vessel for the shared voice of the entire group.

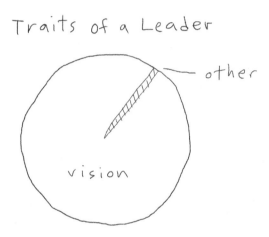

### A Leader sets an example

No matter how a Leader behaves, they're establishing an example that the others on the team will follow whether they realize it or not. Wield that power responsibly. If you're the Leader, you set the tone of the room to begin with, but day after day and meeting after meeting, that tone becomes a company culture. You have the opportunity to make your culture fun and productive just as much as you run the risk of making it sad and lazy. It all depends on the tone you set on a consistent basis, and how hard-working, reliable, dedicated, and kind you choose to be.

### A Leader communicates the system

It's the Leader's job to communicate the system by which the team produces their work. The Leader doesn't necessarily have to be the person who devises the system, they just need to communicate it. They have to give their team their marching orders.(See chapter 9 for the system I recommend.)

**A Leader delegates**

Delegation is one of the most difficult skills for Leaders to adopt. Those who master it can scale big, and usually succeed. Inexperienced Leaders especially have trouble delegating tasks to others because they don't believe anyone else can do a job better than they can do it themselves. If you aspire to lead a team of any size, the sooner you get comfortable with delegating, the better. It will make your job as a Leader much easier.

How to Delegate

*If you're new to delegating, try it. You may find that you're nervous to delegate something important because you're afraid the person you're delegating it to will do a bad job. It's possible they will, but you need to embrace that. Get comfortable allowing the people on your team to fail. Failing is how they learn. Let them fail on something small and noncritical, like organizing your Shortlist, for example (page 74). If they learn and do better on the next try, make it their regular responsibility. When something more important comes up, like finalizing material that will be shown to an audience, you now have more confidence in them, and they have more confidence in themselves. Your trust in them will inspire them to succeed.*

*When delegating, it's important to give people as few rules and requirements as possible. Give people only the basic information they need to do the task, and then leave them alone to figure out the specifics. This invites them to innovate in the way they do things. It's possible they'll devise a better way to do it than you could have thought of, and that's an improvement you should welcome. It boosts their confidence and makes your team better.*

*If you delegate to someone and they drop the ball, don't do a good job, or fail to improve over two or three tries, you discover quickly that they're not a good candidate for delegation.*

### A Leader knows the team

A Leader should know and understand each member of the team adequately enough to motivate and inspire them. Not everyone is motivated and inspired by the same type of leadership. Billy Wilder, the master filmmaker, once advised that a movie director (comparable in most ways to a writers' room Leader) ought to communicate with each actor differently. The way he would speak to Jack Lemmon when making *The Apartment*, for example, inspired an Academy Award-nominated performance. But the same direction might have repelled Marilyn Monroe on *Some Like it Hot*.

### A Leader is decisive

As President George W. Bush famously said, "I'm the decider." Deciding is what a Leader does. How quickly and how confidently Leaders decide is largely how they're judged by their team. Even a bad decision is respected by a team (as long as bad decisions aren't the norm). What's important to people on a chimpanzee level is that decisions are made quickly and confidently.

Whenever there's a dispute among writers—and there will be—the Leader of the writers' room needs to step in and arbitrate and resolve it quickly, urging the parties to move on to something more productive.

For a quick little decision about whether a line is funny, an instant decision is easy. But if there's a big new idea or choice to be made that could impact everyone on the team in a significant way, a Leader has to gather opinions from the team, get the information necessary to make the decision, and then make it. Team members see too much deliberation before a decision as a weakness, so prolonged decision-making should be avoided. For most decisions, a few minutes is adequate. For big decisions, no more than a day. Not every Leader is ready for the advanced strategies suggested by *The Book of the Samurai*, but we can all aspire to it: it quotes the ancient virtue, "Decisions in life should be made within the space of seven breaths."

### A Leader is compassionate

Tyrants become intoxicated by the power of being the final decision maker and lording it over other people. What Tyrants forget is the importance of compassion. When a Leader of a writers' room is compassionate, fear is not the prime motivating factor for the writers. Instead, respect, trust, and even admiration take precedence. A Leader like Abraham Lincoln is a great example of the power of compassion in a Leader. He was so strong and decisive as commander-in-chief during the Civil War that many in his time called him a tyrant. But he's idolized by history for his compassion.

Another example, though fictional, is Captain Kirk in "The Enemy Within" episode of the original *Star Trek*. Kirk is split into two parts by a transporter malfunction, and his id is separated from his compassionate side. His id to too wild to be responsible enough to command the ship, and his compassionate side is too weak and indecisive. Only when Scotty fixes the transporter at the end of the episode, causing Kirk's two halves to be combined, does the captain become a great Leader again, embodying both boldness and compassion.

In a writers' room, a Leader shows compassion by ensuring that everyone's voice is heard, including the Loner's. They also show compassion by encouraging a writer to keep trying if a joke doesn't work, instead of ridiculing them. They show it by actively listening to everyone's opinions, not just about the comedy but about procedural matters. They show it by putting their ego aside, and giving credit to other writers who produce great work. They show it by elevating everyone's ideas, making it clear they value all contributions, not just their own. If they're part of a larger organization, they show it by advocating for the writers with management in all areas.

### A Leader is confident

As you'll see in chapter 14, context is arguably the single most important feature of successful comedy. A key component of context (when it comes to performance comedy or leadership) is confidence. A Leader with confidence will have no trouble making decisions and passing judgment on the comedy before them. If a Leader doesn't have confidence, all of their decisions will be suspect. Not many on the team will rally behind them. A weak and uncertain Leader disheartens and undermines the team. If team members sense a leadership vacuum, the more naturally confident or assertive among them will begin jockeying for power, possibly unseating the Leader.

If you're faced with the prospect of being the Leader of a writers' room, and you don't have confidence, you have to find it—fast. The first way to find confidence, quite simply, is to pretend you have it. This may be difficult; most people can tell when someone's scared but merely acting confident. But don't let this reaction stop you. Even someone pretending to be confident is met with vastly more respect than someone who is overtly timid. Most displays of confidence among chimps are bluffs and bluster. It's seldom real confidence. Humans are no different. You need to muster the hot air and artificially puffed-out chest necessary to pretend you're confident. Keep it up, and in a matter of time, the confidence will become real.

> FUNNIEST-WRITING TIP #7: FAKE IT TILL YOU MAKE IT
> *One of the simplest little secrets of great leadership is that all you have to do to build the confidence to lead is fake it till you make it. Just hold your body in a powerful posture, a Leader's posture. Pretend that you know what you're doing and that you deserve to be in charge, and then act accordingly. This may feel very unnatural if you've never done it before, but it works. Do it enough, and pretty soon you won't be faking it anymore; you'll actually be a confident Leader. Confidence comes from hot air. A lot of leaders in the business world and in politics actually have no qualifications or competence or the proper intelligence to lead, yet they lead anyway because they've faked it enough. If you actually possess the skills and competence necessary to justify your being in charge, you have a leg up. In that case, only a dash of hot air at the start will be necessary.*

The second way to find confidence is by doing all of the other seven actions above. (For more strategies to bolster confidence and combat its terrible opposite, stage fright, see chapter 15.)

CHAPTER 7 ACTION STEP

*Whether you're the Leader of your writers' room or merely a Helper who's been given the opportunity to guest lead, practice embodying the qualities in this chapter the next time your group meets.*

8

# LET ME HELP

"Suck-up." "Teacher's pet." "Brown noser." These are some of the sneering monikers that are whispered behind the back of the Helper when a writers' room gets toxic. Fear of these labels is what prevents a lot of insecure writers from assaying the Helper role, even when they know it's a smart strategy to advance their career or improve the quality of the team's output.

Let jaded writers call you what they want behind your back. It's nothing but jealous, petty chimp behavior that's best ignored. If you cave to your self-doubts and stay out of the Helper role to avoid hurt feelings, you'll get the short-term benefit of not being called a name by an embittered writer or two, but you'll lose out on the long-term benefit of making the writers' room far more productive. You'll also lose out on your best chance to succeed personally.

Helpers succeed. Helpers are all about success. This is a natural role in the writers' room for someone who's ambitious, who wants to climb up the ladder as quickly as possible.

Peter Koechley was an excellent Helper at *The Onion* in the late '90s. While still in high school, he lobbied for a role as an intern and became *The Onion*'s first. His excellent work ethic and pleasant attitude made him a perfect fit for the job. He did whatever was necessary in the writers' room to make sure the process ran smoothly, offering to help the Leader as well as anyone else on the writing staff who needed assistance. He didn't bring his ego to work. He was humble. He had a "service" mindset.

Not surprisingly, Peter went on to be promoted to the role of contributor, then staff writer, and finally, managing editor. After he left *The Onion*, he founded UpWorthy.

Peter's story is common among Helpers. While other comedy writers avoid the Helper role because they feel it's beneath them, those who embrace it go far.

Specifically, the role of Helper entails being of service to any other member of the group, or to the group as a whole, but it focuses primarily on serving the Leader. The Helper attempts to make the Leader's job easier in any way possible. This could mean being the first to volunteer for any delegated responsibilities, the first to propose improvements to the process (but never pushing too hard if the Leader or the majority of the room isn't interested), and it means working hard. Quantity of comedic output should never be more than a friendly competition, but the Helper always strives to deliver at least the amount expected, and usually more.

The best Helper embodies all the qualities of the Leader, specified in chapters 6 and 7. The only difference between the Helper and the Leader is that the Helper is not in charge, nor does the Helper act as if they're in charge. The Helper always defers to the Leader.

The Helper models ideal writers' room behavior: they strive to check their ego; they're supportive and compassionate; they have integrity; they focus on quality; they adopt the same vision as the Leader. The Helper also helps the Leader exemplify and communicate the vision to the rest of the group. The Helper works hard to resist their own chimpanzee instincts, and helps quell those of other group members.

The only time the Helper should not mirror the Leader's vision is in the specific critiques of jokes. The Helper is most helpful to the Leader and to the group effort by focusing on quality, which can't come from slavish adherence to whatever the Leader thinks. Focusing on quality means a relentlessly honest and subjective critique of every concept, aligning with the guidelines for a feedback group spelled out in *How to Write Funnier*. Sometimes the Helper will strongly disagree with the Leader on matters of comedic judgement, and such disagreement is not only acceptable, it's also vitally important.

The Helper should also be welcome, in private meetings, to critique the Leader's process and leadership style. This type of "managing up" should never be done in front of the group, as it would undermine the Leader's authority. But in private, a secure Leader should welcome constructive feedback from the Helper. Improving the process or improving the Leader's behavior in this way directly leads to an improvement in the quality of the group's output.

Predictive amount of
future comedy success

Leader   Helper   Joker   Loner   Drag

Conversely, a Helper would do well to avoid praising the Leader publicly. The Helper should absolutely praise other members on the team when they succeed, but praise for the Leader should only be done in private. Only rarely is it appropriate for a Helper to heap praise on the Leader in front of everyone. If a Helper does this, they become Smithers on *The*

*Simpsons*, which will only invite ridicule from the other writers on the team.

---

FUNNIEST-WRITING TIP #8: IF YOU'RE NOT THE LEADER, BE A HELPER

*No matter what position you hold in the writers' room, if you're not the Leader, be the Helper. Whether you desire the leadership position or not, being the Helper puts you in the best possible position to become the Leader. If you don't want to be the Leader, it at least puts you in the second-best position to affect the quality of the material that the room produces. It also puts you in the second-best position to steer the meeting away from toxic behavior. No matter what the culture of the group, by brazenly offering help, being positive, and focusing on quality, you can transform any writers' room. It also best positions you for your own career advancement, whether on the team you're in, or on the team you aspire to join.*

---

The most important aspect of being a Helper is that their help creates a measurable improvement in the comedy being produced by the group. By reducing the Leader's burden, lessening the Leader's stress, and assisting the Leader in any area needed, the Helper smooths the way for more brainstorming, more riffing, and more productive discussions about what material works and what doesn't. At the same time, by their mere presence, the Helper becomes a subconscious enforcer of the room's culture. The Helper minimizes strife and emotional outbursts, and helps keep everyone focused on creating the funniest possible comedy.

Another aspect of being a Helper worth noting is the benefit to the Helper themselves. Helpers are Leaders in training.

CHAPTER 8 ACTION STEP

*If you're not the Leader of a writers' room, or if you don't want to be one, focus on being the best Helper you can be.*

# 9

# THE MEETINGS

$J$ust like a society needs a system of laws and customs, a comedy writers' room needs a system of best practices. What follows is the protocol for generating the funniest jokes from any writers' room and avoiding the pitfalls.

The Action Steps in the preceding chapters challenged you to start your own writers' room and experience it without any guidelines. This is a valuable experience for any Leader or member of a writers' room. If you followed those steps, you've observed weaknesses in your own behavior as well as the behavior of other members of the team. You've identified the typical roles within a writers' room, and you've likely arrived at your own system for generating content.

Every group needs its own unique procedure. Every project is different, every medium is different, there are different levels of demands on team members' schedules, different budgets, and different time constraints. All of these factors will influence the procedure you adopt for the most efficient writers' room.

However, there is a foundational system that this chapter lays out that's battle-tested. Every writers' room would do well to start with this system.

First, some general principles of a good writers' room:

### The writers hold regular meetings

If meetings are sporadic, output will be too sparse to reach the quantity necessary to achieve quality. Also there's a reduced chance of group cohesion when meetings aren't regular, which can negatively impact the development of a group voice. A writers' room should meet weekly at a minimum.

### Meetings are split in two

Every writers' room should have two meetings: an Editor-brain meeting first, and a Clown-brain meeting second. There will be some overlap between the two parts, but a clear split provides the best opportunity for material to be vetted and for the best ideas to emerge. (Details on this split-meeting principle appear later in this chapter.)

### Every writer brings 10 ideas to the Editor-brain meeting

Every writer in attendance should arrive at the meeting with at least 10 written ideas to discuss. These should be short, in the format of a high-concept longline or short one-line jokes that have the potential to be extrapolated into whatever project the group has adopted. If the task at hand is a TV series or a movie, each idea can be slightly longer, perhaps two or three sentences, to fully encapsulate the entire story arc of the idea being pitched.

Comedy is best written in private, not in a group. Team-written comedy rarely translates into anything useful unless the concept is pre-written by one individual.

No writers' room meeting should commence unless the writers have arrived with ideas to discuss. When comedy ideas are discussed without being pre-written, they're markedly worse, and prone to being "in-jokes." With pre-written ideas, each one can be read aloud to the group, and everyone can experience the First Laugh, which is much more difficult when ideas germinate at the meeting. If no ideas are brought to the meeting, the first 20 minutes of the meeting should be devoted to silent writing time in which each attendee writes 10 ideas for discussion.

> ## THE FIRST LAUGH
>
> *The First Laugh is the only moment in the writers' room that comes close to approximating the audience's experience, which is precious. The First Laugh is when the writers in the room react positively to an idea when it's first uttered. The First Laugh is a singularly important moment for every idea, and capturing that moment is largely the purpose of the first meeting, the Editor-brain meeting. When an idea gets a First Laugh, that laugh should always be remembered and referred to when questioning the viability of the idea in the future.*

### The Leader runs the meetings

The Leader officiates the meetings and delegates tasks to others. Tasks will likely include the following:

• Time-Keeper, in case there's a desired time limit for the meeting. Even with no time limit, it's always a good policy to self-impose a time-limit. A meeting that goes on all day is agonizing for everyone. When a time limit is set, the Time-Keeper can time each section of the meeting to keep the group on task. The Time Keeper keeps the Leader informed about the schedule, and how well it's being followed.

• Shortlist Editor, to take note of the ideas that get a good reaction and seem workable. The Shortlist is the end goal of the first meeting. (More on the Shortlist later in this chapter.)

• Joke Reader, who reads aloud everyone's pre-written concepts brought to each meeting.

• Note Taker or Recorder/Transcriber, to preserve everything that's said in the meeting, for later reference.

### No one pitches their own ideas

The next general principle of a good writers' room is that writers should never pitch their own ideas. The pre-written lists of 10 ideas that writers bring to the first Editor-brain meeting should be handed over to the Joke Reader, who reads each idea, giving everyone's ideas the same weight and keeping the writer of each idea nameless. Discussion should follow any idea that gets a good reaction. If there's elaboration needed on an idea, the writer of the idea can elaborate, but as a rule, it's best to not reveal the identity of the person who conceived the idea until it's been discussed.

Audience Laugh Meter

pitched jokes      pre-written jokes read anonymously

If a writer pitches their own idea, a rash of bias erupts, both for and against the idea, preventing a true capturing of the First Laugh. The group's ability to assess the idea objectively is ruined. The writer will imbue their idea with passion, razzle-dazzle, and salesmanship. They'll use the power of their personality to gin up a good response from the other writers. Will the writer be able to gin up every member of the audience with the same pitch? Of course not. The audience will never see all this salesmanship, so neither should the writers' room. The idea must be presented in as close a form as possible to how the final audience will perceive it. The less fanfare, the better. The idea must succeed on its own merits, not as the result of being pitched by its creator. If an idea is pitched, the funniest ideas will not win the day; only the most successfully pitched ideas will.

**The group discusses ideas that are worthy of discussion**

Most ideas won't be worthy. Ninety percent of everything is garbage, so if nobody likes an idea, the group should abandon discussion and move along to the next pre-written idea. No need to linger. However, riffing is allowed if an idea spurs someone to think of a new idea that gets a good reaction from the group. But in that instance, always be skeptical of the new idea; it's tainted. The room may react positively to it, but that's only because they heard it in the context of the first idea that didn't get a good reaction. The audience won't have this same context.

FUNNIEST-WRITING TIP #9: CAPTURE THE AUDIENCE'S EXPERIENCE

*The writers' room system outlined here is built upon recreating the audience's experience as much as possible. Too often, writers get caught up in their own ideas and forget to connect them back to the end audience, either by veering off take, making ideas unnecessarily complicated, or having too tenuous a connection with their Subtext. If you decide to make any adjustments to this system for your own meetings, err on the side of keeping the audience's experience centered in the minds of the writers. Audiences and writers come from extremely different places. Writers spend far more time with their ideas, care a lot more about them, and are biased heavily toward them. Always treat the First Laugh as sacred. Rely on additional fresh eyes (a second feedback group) whenever you suspect that an idea has become disconnected from its First Laugh. Always keep in mind that the audience is uninvested in your material; they only want to be entertained briefly. You'll often need to look past intense peer pressure in the writers' room to imagine the disinterested audience.*

**Writers have to be heartless in judging ideas**

When pre-written ideas are discussed, writers in the room shouldn't be unduly supportive of their fellow writers' creations. They shouldn't be helpful or positive. They should be heartless. They should be wearing their Editor hats, predisposed to being unimpressed by every idea. They should respond to the idea as if they're the audience: skeptical, selfish, with an attitude that says, "Okay, let's see if you can entertain me." This is an attitude that ferrets out the funniest ideas.

### Ideas that get a good response go on the Shortlist

Any pre-written idea that gets more than half the room to respond favorably goes on the Shortlist, which is a list of the winning ideas that will be discussed at the second meeting.

An idea may be slightly tweaked after discussion—a little tweaking is acceptable—but a major reworking is always perilous. When an idea is altered from its original version, the First Laugh is lost, therefore the room experiences the idea in a different context from the audience.

Conversely, writers' rooms often start with a decent idea and then destroy it by over-workshopping. The idea becomes too complicated, too much of an in-joke, and too far afield from anything that will resonate with an audience. This mistake happens frequently in meetings. The best way to guard against it is to always be wary of ideas that warp into something completely different in the meeting. Such ideas should be vetted by a separate feedback group that isn't in the meeting.

### The meetings run efficiently

A time constraint often looms over meetings. If so, make the meeting efficient by timing the discussion of each joke to fit them all in. For instance, if 30 jokes are brought to the meeting and you have 2 hours, allow only 4 minutes to discuss each joke.

Meetings that go on too long are exhausting. Three or four hours is a good upper limit. If meetings routinely run longer, bring fewer ideas to discuss, or rein in the discussion time for each idea.

The majority of the time in the Editor-brain meeting should be spent listening to and judging ideas. The majority of the time in the Clown-brain meeting should be workshopping, riffing, and finalizing ideas.

Here's a sample rundown of a writers' room meeting:

# THE FIRST MEETING

The first meeting, the Editor-brain meeting, starts with the Leader making any necessary announcements about the status of the project, calling out any especially good work among the team—but not excessively. The wise Leader limits praise to one person (or two people at most) per meeting, otherwise other writers will feel left out. Next, the Leader inspires the group with praise for them and for their efforts as a whole, and expresses confidence in the project's success. A Leader does well to remind the team at this point (or at the end of the meeting) of the overall vision and why they're writing together. This reminder needn't be in every meeting, and it doesn't always have to come at the beginning; it can come at the end too. But the smart Leader continually takes the temperature of the room's morale and gives writers a little pep talk when needed. This entire beginning preamble doesn't need to be any longer than 5 minutes. More than 10 minutes is too much.

Next, the pre-written ideas everyone brought are given to the Joke Reader (unless delivered electronically beforehand). The reader begins reading the ideas. The other writers simply listen. The combined list of pre-written ideas is not given to them. They listen to each idea anew, without any preconceived notions or prejudice, and react as if they're a skeptical audience. The Joke Reader reads each idea clearly but with as little "sell" as possible, just flatly communicating the joke or concept. The Shortlist Editor gauges the room's reaction, and if more than half the room seems to like an idea, it goes on the Shortlist. Or if the Leader wants to overrule a no vote and push an idea, it goes on the Shortlist, but this should be a rare occurrence.

The Editor-brain meeting is made up entirely of the Joke Reader reading ideas. Writers are invited to react to them and judge them as harshly as possible. This is when you'll hear the First Laugh.

There may be some veering into Clown-mode during the first meeting if an idea inspires spontaneous riffing. If that happens, the Leader should dampen enthusiasm and ask everyone to hold their thoughts until the second meeting. The first meeting is for the selection or rejection of ideas only. You waste everyone's time and energy riffing on an idea that may not ultimately be selected.

# THE SECOND MEETING

The second meeting is the Clown-brain meeting. For best results, the second meeting takes place at least a day later. If that's not possible, it can happen after a meal break. Holding the second meeting later allows everyone to get some distance from the ideas discussed in the first meeting, to see them in the light of day, with a Clown hat on instead of an Editor hat.

The Clown-brain meeting begins with a short stint in Editor-brain, with the Joke Reader reading the Shortlist from the previous meeting. The ideas are reassessed. But this time it's not a democratic vote that allows an idea to pass. The Leader makes the decision based on feedback from the room. Some of the ideas will be cut, with the Leader and other writers experiencing "buyer's remorse" after approving the ideas in the previous meeting. Other ideas will stand the test of time and remain viable.

The rest of the meeting is conducted with the writers in Clown-brain mode as they riff freely on the final selected ideas. Everyone throws out jokes and scenarios for how that idea can be escalated and executed. This is when all the writers think and speak like clowns, throwing out any and every idea they have about how to execute the idea. The Leader guides the riffing, keeping everyone on track with the take. Notes are taken (or a recording is made) to ensure that all the riffed jokes are captured.

Next, the Leader assigns any further execution of the idea necessary. If the idea is nothing more than a joke list or short one-liner, it may be all but complete after the riffing. But if it's to be an article, script treatment, or anything longer, the Leader assigns a writer or team of writers the task of writing a first draft with a deadline.

Once the first draft is written, it's brought into a new meeting, and the process starts over: the draft takes the place of the pre-written ideas from the initial Editor-brain meeting. The draft is read without interruption, and the writers provide comments on it. For this second phase of the process, it's not necessary to split the meetings into two parts—they can be part of the same meeting. The group then critiques or riffs on any part of the draft that needs it. The Leader guides the discussion.

The process is repeated for a second draft and beyond until the work is complete.

FUNNIEST-WRITING TIP #10: BEWARE OF ERRANT RIFFING

*In the Clown-brain meeting, when ideas get riffed on, there's a constant danger that riffing will take a wrong turn. Riffing is like a game of telephone, where each idea riffed leads to another thought, which leads to another thought. The writers in the meeting understand the context of the riffs even when they veer far off base. The audience, however, won't have that context. They'll only be aware of the original idea. So if the riffing veers too far afield from the original concept or the best take, the material won't work. The Leader has to be on constant guard against riffing that veers off take, but they must do so without ruining the fun—a tricky balance. A gentle redirect will be necessary from time to time to keep all the riffing on track.*

There are many iterations of this system that can work. Your group could be split into parts, each one with its own Leader. You could have rotating Leaders, where different people lead the first meeting and the second meeting.

Here are the important elements of this protocol to leave intact:

• The hierarchical structure that features a Leader with veto power who's always the final arbiter of the group's comedic voice

 • The approximation of the audience by safeguarding the First Laugh

 • Keeping bias at bay by shielding the identity of the writer of each idea

 • Minimizing political drama with a strong yet compassionate Leader who keeps everyone focused on the task at hand

If you primarily do stand-up, your meeting is the comedy club, and your writers are the audience. You're reading every idea and gauging whether it works based on the audience's reaction. It's a mix of an Editor-brain and Clown-brain endeavor. You're the Leader. Think of the audience as your staff of writers who are there to tell you which jokes work and which don't.

For every other comedy endeavor, this meeting structure will lead to the funniest writing.

# MEDIA-SPECIFIC MEETINGS

Here are specific guidelines for meetings, depending on the media you're working in:

PROSE: Writers bring ideas and titles for written pieces to the Editor meeting. The writers vote on the ideas and any that get more than half the room's approval go on the Shortlist. Once approved, stories from the Shortlist are riffed in the Clown meeting and assigned. Drafts are then brought to a new Editor meeting and discussed. The process is repeated until the writing is final.

WEB SERIES: Writers bring in concepts for the overall series to the Editor meeting, including title ideas. The Shortlist of those ideas is then discussed and riffed on in a later Clown meeting. After a series idea and name are selected, writers bring in ideas for episodes to a new Editor meeting. These ideas are voted on, and the episode-idea Shortlist is discussed at a later Clown meeting, where the winning ideas are riffed on and expanded. Writers are then assigned drafts of episodes that had the most fruitful riffing, using the notes from the riffing session as a guide. They bring those drafts to a new Editor meeting where they're discussed. The process is repeated until the scripts are final.

TV SHOW: Writers bring in concepts for a TV show and those ideas are voted on. Any that get more than half the room's approval go on the

Shortlist. The Shortlist is discussed at the Clown meeting and the Leader selects a winning TV-show idea. If the project begins with a show concept that's been chosen already, writers bring in ideas for episodes. Those episode ideas are voted on, with winners going on the Shortlist. The Shortlist of episodes is then discussed in a later Clown meeting. These should be two-to-three-sentence skeletal descriptions of the episode's complete story (not simply the inciting incident). Once those ideas are vetted through this process, the Leader assigns scripts to writers. Those writers bring those scripts to the next meeting, where the scripts are read, discussed and punched up. This process continues for each script until it's final.

MOVIE: Writers bring loglines to the initial Editor meeting, indicating the entire story of the movie ("Who's fighting Whom, and for What?"). The loglines that make the Shortlist are brought to the Clown meeting, where each longline is riffed on and its story beats fleshed out. The selected concepts are winnowed down and one is chosen. A treatment (1–5 pages long) is assigned to a writer. The writer brings the treatment to an Editor meeting where the treatment is read. This treatment will likely go through several revisions until the story is "broken" (when all the story beats are fleshed out and are working perfectly). Once the story is broken, the full draft of the screenplay can be assigned. The draft is then brought back to an Editor meeting for a reading. The writers give notes on this new draft. The process is repeated until the script is final.

STAGE PLAY: The process for a stage play is the same as the process for a movie.

PODCAST: Writers bring in concepts for the podcast to the Editor meeting, including title ideas. The Shortlist of those ideas is then discussed and riffed on in a later Clown meeting. After a show idea and name are selected, writers bring topic ideas to a new Editor meeting (or episode ideas if it's to be a narrative podcast). The writers vote on these ideas, and any that get more than half the room's approval go on the Shortlist. The Shortlist is discussed at a later Clown meeting, where the winning ideas are riffed on and expanded. Writers are then assigned drafts of episodes that elicited the best riffing, using the notes from the riffing session as a guide. They bring those drafts to a new Editor meeting where they're discussed. The process is repeated until the scripts are final.

STREET ART: Writers bring ideas for street art to the first Editor meeting. Those ideas are voted on, and any that get more than 50 percent of the vote go on the Shortlist. The Shortlist is discussed at a later Clown meeting, where the ideas are riffed on and discussed, and a winning idea and strategy are planned.

VISUAL: Writers bring written descriptions of the visuals to the first Editor meeting. Or, if the budget allows, they bring crude sketches or animatics. These ideas are discussed and voted on. Ideas that are approved by more than half the team go on the Shortlist. The Shortlist is discussed and riffed on at the next meeting, with writers offering comments on how the visual should be executed. Artists are assigned the final selected ideas.

---

FUNNIEST-WRITING TIP #11: ALWAYS REMEMBER THE PRIMARY GOAL

*The number-one goal in the writers' room is crafting the funniest material. And it's not easy. It's a puzzle you'll be working to solve at every stage in the process. Use all the tools at your disposal: your team of writers reacting to the material; isolating the humor from the creator as much as possible in order to remove personality and subjectivity from the equation; remembering the First Laugh; recreating the experience of the audience as much as possible.*

*It may seem at times that the tide is against you in this goal—there are powerful forces working counter to it: egos, subjectivity, the chimp brains of everyone on the team, and other motivations at odds with finding the funniest material. The challenge is to stay on target, and focus on what will be funny to the audience.*

---

Every project should go through a similar process. The biggest mistake that comedy creators make is becoming attached to a project that hasn't been vetted. If you have a project that you love and want to pursue, don't execute it until you come up with nine more project ideas and meet with other writers who also bring 10 ideas, and then see if your pet idea is the one that wins out after going through the process. This is the best way to make sure that your project, after all the time and money you invest in it, isn't a dud.

CHAPTER 9 ACTION STEP

*Implement the system outlined in this chapter and run your meeting accordingly.*

# A UNITED FRONT

When writing a first draft of a short comedy piece, sketch, or stand-up bit, the writer needs to summon strict discipline to stay on take; temptations to veer off into new, unrelated territory meet the writer at every turn. A similar but broader struggle exists in the writers' room. The Leader needs to stay focused on keeping the room on target. Temptations to descend into bias and chimpanzee behavior meet the group of writers every second.

In the writers' meeting it's easy for everyone in attendance to forget why they're there. At every moment, our baser impulses take over. Without realizing it, we suddenly take on new priorities, like proving our dominance, establishing our significance, and surviving in the social hierarchy.

Use the following list as a reference to remind you of the priorities in every meeting:

**Create the best possible material**

Whether you're the Leader of the group or a ranking member, you might want to put your own stamp on the comedy, consciously or unconsciously. You'll want your idea selected, your riffed joke to be included, and your voice heard.

You need to let go of this harmful desire to be significant. Have confidence in the final result of the meting even if your mark doesn't end up on a particular piece of comedy. Let the energy of the room support the ideas that get the most laughs during idea-voting or riffing. When you stay focused on making sure each idea is promoted, as opposed to the individual promoting it, the meeting stays on track and you allow the best material to rise to the top.

### Put heads together

By listening to more than 50 percent of the group, trusting their judgment, and carefully considering the "no" votes, you create a multi-headed comedy mastermind that thinks as one. The writers' room becomes like a stand-up performance in front of a real audience, which is the most reliable way to determine whether something is funny. But unlike a stand-up performance, a writers' room is a controlled, scientific setting. It's an open-mic night where the charisma of the performer is unable to artificially sell the material. The comedy is isolated and assessed in the most objective possible light.

When a writers' room gels, you create a powerful comedy-creation and comedy-assessment engine. Not only are the assembled writers serving as a makeshift stand-up audience judging the material, but also, they're working to create it using the same high standard as the Leader. They're like a comedy-club audience that helps write the comedy.

### Continually improve

When you run a writers' room, you step one foot out of the comedy world and into the management world. Management, as we've learned, is difficult to learn, and only a handful of business leaders ever learn to do it well. But one simple tip that can improve any manager's performance is to focus on continual improvement.

Continual improvement is one of the most important tenets of Total Quality Management, a system developed by W. Edwards Deming and popularized by management guru Peter Drucker. Stasis comes easily to any endeavor, so an active focus on improvement is essential to growing an audience.

In comedy, we tend to go with what works—what's bankable. We get lazy, we use recurring templates, and we fall into clichés easily. But the one essential ingredient in comedy is surprise. And the audience won't be surprised if the comedy is always the same. You need to keep improving it.

Beyond the comedy, you want to keep an eye out for ways to improve your meeting protocol as well. Refine your meetings to suit the individual needs of your comedy project. Make your meetings even more of a meritocracy, more streamlined, less emotional, and less inclined to descend into chimp behavior.

### Focus on the audience

The writers in the room are indeed a substitute audience, but they're not a real audience. Sometimes what people get excited about in a writers' room will fall flat in front of a real audience. Everyone at the meeting has to constantly put themselves in the shoes of the audience. This can be helpful in determining whether material will ultimately be perceived as funny. The audience's context will always be different from yours. They're not sitting in that writers' room, after all. So, the writers have to be aware of the audience's context and always keep it clearly in mind, judging the final work through that lens.

Comedy writers want to have fun writing comedy. But often, comedy writing is not fun; it's hard work. Many beginning comedy writers make the mistake of thinking that if they're having fun, the audience will have fun too. The opposite is more often true, especially in the early stages of crafting material. However, when material is in its final form, you'll know when you have good material if the writers seem surprised by how much they enjoy it. If they suddenly act as if they're an audience who's never seen or heard it before, taking it in hungrily and laughing, seeming like they forgot that they themselves wrote it, you've done a good job, and the audience will probably have a similar reaction.

**Be apolitical**

The politics among any group of people has the potential to get toxic. Differing opinions about the material are usually easy to smooth over, but situations where people don't get along or find themselves competing in an unhelpful way are more difficult. The Leader must never play favorites, and must always work to quell any discussion unrelated to comedy that causes discomfort or tension in the room. A foundational feature of your culture should be that you treat everyone with equal respect. Give ideas from every individual the same consideration without indulging interpersonal conflicts.

> FUNNIEST-WRITING TIP #12: THE AUDIENCE IS ALWAYS RIGHT
>
> *In comedy, there's only one rule: the audience is always right. If they laugh, it's funny; if they don't, it's not. In the writers' room, your audience is made up of the writers. There are numerous factors that influence whether a real audience laughs, and as a comedy creator you want to take control of every factor: the quality of the writing, the context of the delivery, the delivery itself, and the state of the audience. In the writers' room, almost all those factors can be eliminated, giving you a hermetically sealed environment that judges work with almost pure objectivity. In this case, your writers become the perfect test audience.*

# CHARACTERISTICS OF A WRITERS' ROOM

When the goals above are woven into the room's culture, you create a writers' room that takes on these winning characteristics:

**The writers are serious about even the appearance of a cliché**

The search-and-destroy mission a comedy writer conducts against clichés' or any kind of unoriginality should be heightened in a writers' room.

You heighten this mission by focusing not just one mind, but several, on ferreting out material that seems too similar to other material being produced by other comedy writers. This one mission will do more to sharpen the unique comedic voice of the room than almost anything else, and it will ensure that the comedy that comes out of it is as original as possible.

### The writers are serious about saying the right thing

Comedy is often deconstructed in a good writers' room. The writers will discuss the Subtext behind their comedy, the wording, and why it works. These are worthy discussions. Writers need to be aware of what their comedy is saying, and they need to be able to stand behind it. If they're not saying anything, or they're saying something that doesn't sit right with the group or the Leader, they need to be conscious of their failing, and right the ship. The Subtext that typically comes out of a writers' room is an important component of the group's unique comic voice. It comes from the personalities and souls of the writers who are a part of it, and everyone needs to feel a sense of integrity about what message they're sending out into the world.

### The writers are serious about comedy

There's always some joviality in a meeting of comedy minds, but it's rarely frivolous. Creating comedy is serious work, and the writers take it seriously. In the end, comedy creation is an intellectual process. When writers realize this, joviality and laughs result, but not necessarily in the writers' room. The laughter comes later, when it truly matters, to the audience.

# WHAT MAKES A GOOD PROJECT?

How do you choose a good project for your writers' room to tackle? To address this critical question, use the same process for generating concepts to write on your own: come up with lists of ideas, and then use a feedback group (in this case, the writers' room itself) to help select the project. A lot will depend on what you and your group's interests are, but here are some general things to shoot for:

### It's sustainable

If it's an ongoing project, like a weekly podcast, you want to make sure there's enough interest to keep it going.

### It's affordable

Will the project require a budget? If so, where will the money come from? The best projects start with little or no money, only passion. Only when the project finds its footing—and an audience—should you consider investing money in it.

### It's easy to produce

Depending on the medium of your project, the burden of production can bring down everyone's spirits. Keeping the project simple is a good idea, especially in the beginning.

### It's original

If you ever hope to make a splash with your project, make sure it's unlike anything else. Originality is one of the most important keys to success in comedy.

# HOW TO INCORPORATE YOUR WRITERS' ROOM

If your writers' room is creating something for sale, or something that has the potential to be sold, or is an asset that could someday have monetary value, a good idea to consider is creating an official business structure for the group.

Every room is different. Consult a copyright lawyer for advice on your situation if you want to make sure you're making the best decisions for you. This section provides some basics to keep in mind to prevent serious problems down the road.

Determine who owns the intellectual property. Does the Leader own all the comedy material that the group creates? Or does each individual member of the team own their part of the work? According to U.S. and E.U. copyright laws, as soon as you create a piece of writing, it becomes your intellectual property, and either you or your estate own it until 70 years after you die. But when you're working as part of a group, whoever structures the group usually makes a different arrangement.

Trying to divide ownership among several people who work together on a piece of intellectual property can be incredibly messy. The simplest way to handle the matter is to make a decision about who owns the material beforehand. The Leader (or in the case of a larger organization, the person who hired the Leader) may decide to own it, giving them the power to decide how it's distributed and monetized. This would be done by creating a corporate structure such as a Limited Liability Company (LLC) (which, in the U.S., involves paying a fee and registering a company name with the secretary of state in your state. For other countries, consult a lawyer to determine your best course of action). For a larger organization with paid employees, an S-corp or C-corp might be a more practical way to organize. Consult an accountant for advice on how to structure your organization for maximum tax benefit.

The LLC or corporation needs a name, and it needs agreements with everyone involved spelling out how the individual writers who contribute to the material will be compensated. A good step to take with both an LLC and a corporation is to require everyone on the team to sign a "work for hire" agreement, acknowledging that they understand who owns the work they're contributing to, if it's not them.

A wise Leader offers contributing writers a share in the eventual profits earned from the work, especially if there's no upfront payment. A wise contributing writer asks for a share of the profits even if they're offered payment upfront.

CHAPTER 10 ACTION STEP

*Check your meeting against the points in this chapter to make sure it's organized properly and has its priorities straight.*

# 11

# THRIVE IN ANY ROOM

Blane loved comedy. He wanted to be a professional someday. Sometimes he'd daydream about being a writer on *SNL*. Other times he'd picture being a famous stand-up comic, maybe hosting *SNL*.

Blane's problem was that he didn't work very hard at it. He didn't feel motivated to write very often, so his output was sparse and lackluster. Because he didn't produce a lot of comedy, he was slow to get better at it, and he got no closer to his goal of getting into the comedy business.

Deep down, although Blane loved comedy, he knew he wasn't trying very hard. He always had a difficult time sitting down and writing anything funny. He believed what he needed was some kind of external accountability.

One day Blane got the idea of joining a writers' group that met once a week. A group, he imagined, would shore up his weaknesses. They would provide the cover he needed. Maybe in the group, he thought, his comedy would shine. Some of the funnier people in the group would give him a lift and inspire him to be better, he figured, like with improv. He also thought being in the group would give him much-needed motivation to sit down and write.

Joining a group would be good for Blane, but unless the group is all made up of dabblers at his level, he would not be good for the group.

A group is strongest when every member is the best writer they can be, is motivated to produce material on their own, and sharpens their craft so they contribute the best possible skills.

A writers' room should be a "dream team" of the best comedy writers who can be cajoled to join it. A weak member like Blane who's not pulling their weight will drag down the entire group. Some writers may be less experienced than others—that's understandable. But every writer should be just as capable, just as hardworking, and just as dedicated as everyone else.

Cultivate the following characteristics to make the most of any writers' room you're in:

### Be honest

Honesty in a writers' room is critical, especially in your feedback on comedy writing. Don't ever fake a positive response to a joke. A genuine opinion about comedy is the only one that matters because it's the only one that approximates the audience. If you're glossing over your true opinion, you're playing a chimp game of sparing someone from hurt or trying to gain favor with an alpha. Be cautious of this easy mistake and avoid it.

However, criticism should be delivered tactfully, at least until you've established a certain comfort level with your cohorts. In some writers' rooms, outright expressions of "that sucks" are discouraged. In others, blunt language is part of how the writers communicate and produce great work. Read the room, and when in doubt, always be diplomatic when you don't like an idea. Say, "It's not really working for me, but maybe we could brainstorm ways to make it work," or "Normally your ideas are amazing, Chris, but this one's not really doing it for me." Employ the "shit sandwich" method of criticism, where a negative thought is encased between two compliments. The shit sandwich is always a good strategy when criticizing.

FUNNIEST-WRITING TIP #13: A WRITERS' ROOM IS NOT A FREE RIDE

*A lot of writers like working in a group for the wrong reason: they want to hide in the group. They figure their weaknesses as comedy writers will be shored up by brighter minds in the group.*

*While it's true that a good writers' room will elevate everyone in it to create humor at the top of their intelligence, it's a mistake to go into a group knowing you're a weak link. You're only bringing the group down. A group works best when each participant operates at a high skill level.*

*An example of this principle in action is the writing team of* The Dana Carvey Show, *the legendary sketch show deemed too funny for prime-time TV. It featured a dream writing staff: Stephen Colbert, Steve Carell, John Glaser, Louis C.K., Robert Smigel, Charlie Kaufman, Bob Odenkirk, and the writing staff of* The Onion. *Each one of these writers was a spectacular talent in their own right. Together, they were an incredible force of comedy that produced a short-lived show in the '90s that's still talked about in reverent tones today.*

*When you're a prolific writer with a distinct voice, you add exponentially to the group. A certain cohesion takes place that melds individual voices of the same calibre into a new voice. This kind of cohesion is more difficult with a writer or writers on the team whose contributions are under par.*

*Just like a person can't walk very well with one leg asleep, neither can a writers' room soar if one or more members is unable to keep up.*

Beyond being honest about the jokes, strive to be honest in your personal communication as well. Don't pretend to be someone you're not. Be authentic, tell the truth, and don't worry about being judged. Those kinds of worries are in the chimp domain, and they won't serve you. You may not get everyone to like you—that's nearly impossible in any scenario—

but if you're always honest, you'll at least get their respect.

**Work the hardest**

You don't want to be overtly competitive in a writers' room, but you do want to raise the bar in subtle, nonthreatening ways. If the assignment is to arrive at the meeting with 10 ideas, bring 12. If there's an accepted standard of quality for how written material is presented to the group, make yours a little more polished. Always be on time, or a little early.

**Be politically savvy**

Be attuned to the relationships between the people on the team and be mindful of their political games, alliances, petty squabbles, and competitions. Always endeavor to rise above such things but be aware of them. Being aware of the political landscape will allow you to motivate people better, especially if you're angling to become the Leader.

comedy staff writer job requirements

resumé        jokes        Being great to work with

**Be the Leader or the Helper**

Always be the Helper in every writers' room, no matter what kind of room it is. And whenever possible, be the Leader. This may entail simply offering to be a Helper to the existing Leader or to the Leader's boss. Being a Helper or Leader will put you in the best position to influence everyone else on the team, make positive improvements to the process, and make the funniest comedy.

**Be great to work with**

Beyond being hardworking, productive, and dedicated to the overall quality of the team's output, you need to make a conscious effort to be a great co-worker. That means being nice, supportive, and pleasant. Go along with the team. Inspire other members of the team to say, "Boy, that person is a delight to work with!" A great way to start is by practicing the line items in chapters 6, 7 and 8. Even if you're not the head writer or editor of a writers' room, act like a Leader in any way that doesn't usurp or threaten the actual Leader. This, in combination with being the best writer you can be as an individual, will make you great to work with.

# HOW TO GET HIRED ON A WRITING TEAM

If you want to be on a writing team, the most effective way to demonstrate your worthiness is to work hard, work smart, and dedicate yourself. A job on a professional writing staff will demand these things. Before a professional writers' room takes you on, they want to know if you're hardworking and smart. They'll determine your qualifications by reading your submission, watching any comedy you've produced online, and interviewing you. They also want to know you're dedicated. They'll determine your dedication by taking note of how active you are with your comedy. Do you perform stand-up or improv? Do you publish comedy articles in magazines or online? Are you making funny YouTube videos? Are you doing all of the above? If you are, they're far more likely to judge you a good fit for their writers' room.

There are different kinds of writers' rooms, as we saw in chapter 4. If you're trying to get selected to be on a writing team, you won't know in advance what kind of room it'll be. But if you can maintain the right attitude, you'll thrive in any writers' room, no matter how dysfunctional. Your effort will pay off in myriad ways: you'll have a better chance of landing a spot on the team, you'll make the team better, and you'll get placed in another (perhaps better) writers' room if you ever want an upgrade.

You may be concerned that some of the behavior recommended in this chapter might make other writers, especially your co-workers, resent you. This concern is not unfounded. You might earn some writers' resentment. But that's a lesser evil than a writer's disrespect, which you'll surely earn if you're like Blane—a drag on the team. When you perform at your best in the meeting, you'll help not only your own career but the entire team's performance. Being "average" in a group may satisfy some chimp instincts to blend in, in certain rooms where writers don't work very hard, but that approach is nothing more than short-term pain avoidance. As long as you're great to work with, friendly, and honest, you'll keep any resentment at a minimum while at the same time doing right by your team, yourself, and your future.

FUNNIEST-WRITING TIP #14: BE GREAT TO WORK WITH

*Be cheerful, unflappable, and positive. Volunteer for things, express your honest opinion, and be nice to the people on your team. Offer to hangout with them after the meeting. Support them in their work. Offer praise liberally, and always share credit for success. Work on your craft to be as good a team member as you can be. Work the hardest, but never aggressively compete. Being great to work with is the best insurance you can have against losing a writing staff job, and it's your best chance to secure promotion into the ranks of leadership or into other writers' rooms in the future.*

## CHAPTER 11 ACTION STEP

*Focus on each actionable behavior in this chapter to be the best writer in whatever group you're in.*

# 12

# TAKING THE STAGE

If you've only been reading up to this point and not practicing, the concepts in this book may seem simple. Implementing the meeting protocol and best practices outlined here may seem like a smart and worthy idea, and you may be thinking you'll get around to trying it next time you have a meeting.

But if you haven't done the action steps yet, if you haven't tried running a writers' room of any kind, you're missing out on a key factor of how it all works.

This is not just an intellectual exercise; it's an emotional one. Your chimp brain is powerful. When you run a meeting of writers for the first time, it's like trying stand-up comedy for the first time. Your chimp brain will scream foul and you won't know what hit you. You'll get butterflies. You'll be visibly nervous and unsure. You'll lack confidence. You'll be a lot worse at it than you expect. Your own personal weaknesses will bubble up and take over. You'll make embarrassing mistakes. And you'll do poorly even if you've read this book several times and memorized key passages about how to lead a writers' room.

No one can take charge of a meeting and run it like a pro the first time, even after filling their head with all the book-learning in the world, just like no one can get on stage and do perfect stand-up after reading a book. Life doesn't work that way. Everybody's different and everybody has different fears and failings. These are skeletons you have to clear out of your emotional closet on your own. The only way to truly get good at running a writers' room—and stand-up—is to practice. A lot.

If you haven't done the action steps in all the chapters so far, please go back and do them. Set up a weekly meeting schedule with your feedback group and stick to it.

As you practice, refer back to this chapter to see if any of your challenges are addressed. Here are the most common stumbling blocks an inexperienced Leader might face when trying to run a writers' meeting, and how to avoid them:

### You're more of a Tyrant than you realize

Depending on your personality, you may veer into Tyrant behavior without realizing it. You'll favor your ideas over others'. You'll announce how you feel about each idea before hearing from anyone else in the group, not realizing this undermines their confidence. You'll subtly suggest that your opinion is more important than theirs. You'll neglect to ask a quiet member of the group for their feedback.

This scenario happens a lot: a concept is brought up that a majority of the group likes. Writers start talking over each other, riffing on the idea, laughing, and getting swept away. A lone writer, a Loner, gets caught up in the riffing too, and starts to say something. They get two or three words out at most, but the other people are talking so loudly and quickly that the Loner is drowned out. You, the Leader, are laughing and riffing along with the others, and you don't notice the Loner. Meanwhile, the Loner feels slapped down, like no one cares to hear their riff, and they may never speak up again. You'll lose all the potentially hilarious jokes they might have contributed.

Ultimately you do in fact have veto power, but it costs you nothing to hear the reactions of everyone on the team first. Then—and only then—weigh in with the final decision. This small distinction can make the difference between a Tyrant and a Best Boss. Always be mindful of each member of your team. Make sure no one is excluded from the conversation. If you see a scenario like the above, interrupt the riffing to ask the Loner what they were going to say, and then give them positive feedback for their contribution, regardless of whether you thought it was good. This will make them feel like a valued member of the team and empower them to open up and contribute more.

### You're too nervous

You'll try to mask your nervousness, but people will notice. They'll notice your shaky hands, your quavering voice, or your flop sweat. If you get nervous, the most important thing to realize is that everyone gets nervous. Simply acknowledging to yourself and even to the group that you're nervous is a good way to push past it

There are ways to minimize nervousness. You can come prepared—not scripted, but with a confident grasp of the system you intend to communicate. You can pause, take a deep breath, or take a drink of water. You can adopt a confident posture, which can trick your brain into thinking you're actually confident. You can keep in mind that most of the meeting will not be you speaking in front of a group; it will be you listening to the other writers expressing their opinions and then you chiming in with your verdict, based mostly on simply reacting to their opinions. You can practice in a mirror or on video so you're aware of how you look, the way you speak, or anything else about yourself that makes you feel self-conscious.

Take comfort in knowing that it's only going to get better next time. Do your best and plough through. This is a sink-or-swim moment; no matter how desperate you think you look, as long as you forge ahead, you're swimming, not sinking. Just stay focused and get the job done, nervousness be damned. (For more techniques to bolster your confidence in front of a group, see chapter 15.)

### You're too petty

You may be overly focused on a perceived slight, or on an unimportant matter. This will erode the group's confidence in you as the Leader. People like to see their Leader focused on the big picture without getting bogged down in small things, especially when those things are emotional squabbles. Getting involved in such things makes a Leader look weak. People have a deep instinct to follow a strong Leader, not a weak one.

### You're too conciliatory

If you're too conciliatory, your meeting will devolve into a committee. You'll lack the backbone to make bold decisions, break tie votes, and make a strong stand when, for example, you take the side of a minority opinion, or make a decision about an important aspect of the project that faces strong disagreement. The more a writers' room devolves into a committee, the more your team will lose respect for you as a Leader. They'll begin to think they don't need a Leader. And a committee-run meeting with no Leader will result in weaker comedy without a consistent voice.

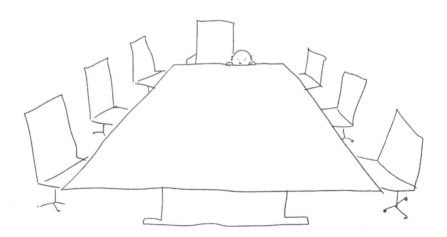

### You're too quiet

A common mistake a lot of beginning Leaders make is that they're too mousy. They don't make their presence adequately known in the meeting. They retreat into the background and let discussions go on without them.

A Leader should always be managing the discussion, moving it along, and staying on top of it. Comedy writers have a tendency to wander off topic. The Leader brings things back to the task at hand and needs a clear, strong voice to do so. Your authority as a Leader diminishes when you're quiet. People's natural instinct is to follow the loudest and most passionate person in the room. You don't necessarily have to out-shout everyone, but you do need to be a presence, and you need to stay engaged. Your level of involvement and passion (not volume) should at least be on the same level as the most boisterous writers in the room.

FUNNIEST-WRITING TIP #15: DISCUSSING IS NOT RIFFING
*Sometimes when riffing on concepts, writers will simply be discussing the joke, musing about why it works or doesn't work, or deconstructing it. They may even start talking about a subject scarcely related to the joke at all. They won't actually be suggesting joke beats or story beats based on the concept. It's the Leader's job to gently prod writers away from this kind of unproductive discussion and toward suggesting ideas for joke beats, story beats, or audience expectations for the concept. These are the only things that provide the raw material that the meeting must produce.*

Failing to speak up and failing to make your presence known gives your team an opening to question who's in charge. And as the Leader, you always want to show that you're the one in charge (with subtle actions more than words).

### You fail to resolve conflict decisively

Failing to resolve conflicts is a common problem for beginning Leaders. A disagreement—even a slight disagreement that's conducted politely—will bubble up in the group, and you'll fail to handle it. You'll fail to keep people focused on the task at hand. You'll fail to diffuse any lingering tension. Often all that's required to relieve such tension is to smooth it over with some humor, acknowledge the feelings of all parties, or remind everyone of the shared goal. For a major dispute, talking it through is an important step to finding resolution. The Leader's job is to resolve conflict and keep the meeting on target.

All eyes are on you when you're the Leader. That fact will worsen most of the failings listed in this chapter. You'll make subtle gestures that the other writers will perceive that you may not be aware of. They'll imbue your smallest gestures with nefarious meaning. For this reason and others, the experience of running a meeting is impossible to glean from reading a book.

In real life, under stress, your inner chimp will come crashing to the forefront of your mind. Only through practice can you build habits that keep chimp behavior at bay.

CHAPTER 12 ACTION STEPS

*1. When you're leading a meeting, be mindful of your own tendency to slip into the behavior described in this chapter.*

*2. Make notes after each meeting, recounting what you did well and what you didn't do well.*

# 13

# GOING VIRTUAL

When governments began instituting lockdowns during the Pandemic in early 2020, comedy creators who relied on regular writers' room meetings scrambled to create virtual writers' rooms. Live performers saw their income plummet.

Before Covid-19, many creators who didn't have the financial means, or were spread across distances, were already making use of virtual writers' rooms to create comedy. *McSweeney's Internet Tendency* is one example, where editors in various locations review submissions from writers all over the world, provide notes by email, and then publish online.

There are a number of different ways to set up a successful virtual writers' room. Solo performers can also harness the "writers' room" of the live audience in a number of different ways.

To create the books *Trump's America: Buy This Book and Mexico will Pay for It* and *Welcome to the Future Which Is Mine*, I assembled small teams and conducted virtual writers' rooms.

For *Trump's America*, the writers held in-person meetings in the fall of 2015 to settle on the project: a book about what it would be like if Donald Trump became president. We then held Editor meetings to amass ideas for the book and vote on the best ideas to pursue. There were some 25 total writers. Some served as section editors. I served as Leader. We met in person once every month or two, but largely created the book over email, with writers sending ideas to me. I would then assign articles, listicles, and graphics. A virtual Clown meeting was held afterward, involving my getting feedback on the drafts from subgroups of writers, all by email. I edited and finalized the copy, and then sent it to a proofreader and graphic designer. The mostly virtual process was smooth and efficient.

The team for *Welcome to the Future Which is Mine* was smaller, less than 10 writers. I again served as Leader. It was a less ambitious book, so it didn't need as much coordination as *Trump's America*. There were no in-person meetings (at least, not until the book release party). Writers first submitted ideas for sections, chapters, and essays. I selected the winners after the team voted through email. I then broke the team into writers and editors. Section editors edited different features in the book, while writers focused on generating jokes for graphics and listicles. After the writers and editors delivered the material, I made a final editing pass and sent it to the publisher.

During the early months of the Pandemic, stand-up comics like Erica Rhodes performed to virtual audiences on Zoom, which allowed them (and their audiences) to hear the laughs. Comedian Ben Bailey performed comedy regularly from his Facebook page, getting live comments from viewers during the performance.

Tapping into the laugh-based opinion of a live audience has traditionally been the only way for a comedian to test new jokes. With live online performances, they can now see the audience react with comments and emojis.

Comedians with more than 30,000 subscribers to their YouTube channel (the current requirement) can also perform live on YouTube and enable "super chat," which allows the audience to tip the performer as well as comment during livestreams.

Zoom, which has been widely adopted for non-comedy meetings, is an effective option for writers' room meetings. Transcribing a virtual meeting becomes a breeze with platforms like Zoom that offer replay recordings of the meeting. No First Laugh will be forgotten and no riffed joke will be lost.

THE VIRTUAL WRITERS' ROOM

*A writers' room doesn't need to be an in-person meeting to generate the funniest possible humor. In fact, a virtual writers' room is often more effective at curtailing the chimp instincts typically at play in an in-person meeting. With everyone physically separated, the writers are more like "brains in a jar" rather than chimps in a subgroup. Virtual meetings can be held on a conference call or on video chat, with each providing some hope of capturing the First Laugh. These formats also allow for riffing that takes advantage of people's improv skills. Chimp behavior might still bubble up on a video call, but it's easier to quell without heated, in-person energy.*

*Another virtual writers' room is no meeting at all. A Leader can simply ask writers to send in ideas and vote on them by email, with the Leader assessing the final ideas from the Shortlist and getting email feedback from the group after making selects. An email nonmeeting like this almost completely eliminates chimp behavior. One drawback is that it becomes difficult to use chimp instincts to the Leader's advantage, such as establishing authority, bonding, and overall cohesion.*

Voting can be more systematic in a virtual meeting, with each writer chiming in with chat or through email. They won't be swayed by the votes of others, which can often be a problem in in-person meetings. Sub-par jokes (jokes that might face harsher judgement in a virtual meeting) can sometimes squeak through the approval process in an in-person meeting due to peer pressure. A virtual meeting avoids this problem.

The system for running a writers' room spelled out in chapter 9 is pliable. It can be adjusted to fit any meeting scenario. Meetings can still be split into two parts, the Editor meeting and the Clown meeting. The Editor meeting is a natural fit for going virtual. The participants are less able to "read the room," which stirs up all kinds of chimp behavior. They're less likely to be affected by the charisma of a fellow writer who might oversell an idea and artificially inflate it. They're less likely to descend into chimp behavior. And they're more likely to judge material objectively.

Writers can even be encouraged to write silently during a significant portion of a virtual meeting, using it as an accountability tool to regiment time to write.

CHAPTER 13 ACTION STEP

*Try all variations of online meetings to see which ones work best for your group.*

# 14

# ANOTHER SECRET WEAPON

Having a team bolster your comedy is your first secret weapon for creating the funniest possible comedy and rising to the top in the new comedy revolution.

There is another, and it's equally powerful.

Practiced comedy writers and performers instinctively know the right time and place to tell a joke, in person or on the page. And if it's not the right time or place, they know how to twist the context to create the right time and place. They are, in effect, fashioning the perfect soil for their humor seed to bear the fruit of laughs.

People who haven't mastered this skill don't get laughs; they get awkward stares, grimaces, or indifference.

How do the professionals do this? And how can you?

Everything you learned in this book and in the previous books in this series about Subtext, the Funny Filters, and structuring comedy will be useless if you present your material in the wrong context. Put it in the right context, however, and your joke will elicit gales of laughter.

Here's where humor gets its reputation for being subjective. How can a joke be hilarious in one context, and a dud in another?

We all know that comedy material that creates fits of laughter in a nightclub may not go over so well in a church. We also know that a whispered joke that busts up your classmates isn't likely to amuse your geometry teacher in the middle of class.

We've all experienced the feeling of not being in the mood to laugh at anything. Or when humor comes "too soon."

We all know that the way a joke is delivered can mean success or failure.

Setting, emotion, and delivery: All these things can radically shift the context of humor.

If you understand and can skillfully manage the context of your comedy, you can create the leverage you need to tip the playing field in your favor, making audiences experience your humor as objectively funny. This is how the professionals do it, and it's one of the hidden secrets of comedy. Even with all the best-crafted jokes in the world, the comedy writer still needs to set up their audience to laugh.

When you're ready to present your comedy to the world, you're like a parent at a school play, hoping your pride and joy will be met with adoration. This moment, when your funny creation is delivered to your audience, is the point of no return. After that moment, you either get laughs or you don't. Before this point is where the real work of contextualizing happens. Before you ever present something funny, you need to fully comprehend—and if possible, control—its context. Planning ahead can save you from bombing.

# THE CONTEXT PYRAMID

The Context Pyramid shows the most foundational contextual elements at the bottom and the more nuanced ones further up. Before you present a joke to an audience, go through this pyramid. When writing prose, going through this pyramid will be easy; a prose writer has the luxury of time. If you're not primarily a prose writer, practice going through the pyramid using the prose medium. Once you're more comfortable with it, apply it to a more difficult medium, like video or audio. Then, when you've mastered those media, try it on the stage or in person. These media are the most difficult places to use the Context Pyramid because you have to act fast. Such adeptness only comes with practice.

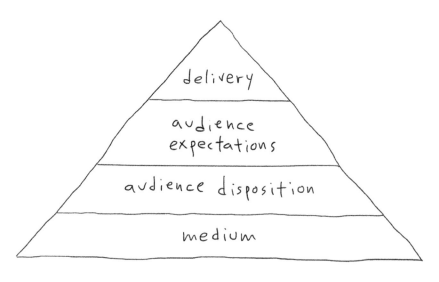

The comedy Context Pyramid

Here's how to go through the pyramid: start at the bottom, assess, and adapt. Then move up to the next level and do the same. Continue assessing at each level, adjusting if necessary, and work your way to the top.

If you can tweak the context in your favor at every level before you get to the top, (the delivery), you'll very likely get a laugh, even if your joke isn't very good. That's the power of context. Mastering context is how so many mediocre comedians and comedy shows succeed. They essentially trick their audiences into laughing.

However, armed with great jokes instead of mediocre jokes, a comedy writer who aces the Context Pyramid will have an extraordinary advantage.

The first layer of the pyramid is the medium. Your material will be perceived differently depending on its medium. Audiences are different for different media. They have different expectations. By choosing your medium wisely, you can control certain aspects of your audience.

In the prose medium, you don't know where your audience is, but you know they want to read something. How can you surprise them in this medium? You do it in the way the prose is presented, how it's laid out, and where it's presented. There are no rules here. You don't have to do it the way everyone else does it. Can you think of a unique way to present your prose? Try it.

One small example of a context shift in prose that gets great results is when an Instagram post features writing on a napkin or some other object in the picture instead of in the description below the picture. A lot of readers are accustomed to just looking at the pictures and skipping over the description copy, but the napkin scrawl puts the writing in a surprising context, and people are magnetically drawn to read it.

In the audio medium, you can assume your audience isn't paying close attention. They might be doing something else, like riding an exercise bike or driving. A shock jock like Howard Stern took advantage of this context and pierced through with the Shock Funny Filter to grab people's attention. The creators of Serial did the same thing but with a different approach. They used the power of dramatic story—uncommon in podcasts—to draw listeners in.

With video, your audience is relaxed and probably in the mood to turn off their brains and watch something. You change the context by showing them something they've never seen before, or something recognizable but with a twist, with fast cutting, or unusual sound to change the tone.

A great example of a context shift in video is the way Bad Lip Reading presents video you've seen, but with their sound.

The audience for movies is absolutely in the mood to watch something, and they expect to be taken on an emotional ride. They expect a spectacle.

With the stage, the audience is also in the mood to watch something, but something immediate, real, and more intimate.

In the visual medium, you may be catching people off guard, depending where you post your visual comedy.

With street art, people don't even realize they're an audience.

Each one of these media creates a different context for humor. A skilled comedy writer adjusts their comedy to each medium in order to control the context. Your medium (some media more than others) will get you part of the way to understanding how your audience feels. Some media have predictable audiences; others don't, and in that case you need to influence the audience's disposition, the second layer of the pyramid.

The format of prose affects how potential readers feel about it. *The Onion* uses the format of a serious news website. This puts the audience in a serious mood, setting them up for a big surprise when they discover that the material is funny. A crowd in a comedy club or at a comedy movie is primed to laugh due to the theater environment. Comedians and comedy filmmakers use this context to their advantage. It's why they present their work in a theater and not on a street corner. An audience for street art may not be in the mood to laugh. Bill Murray, the master of the street art medium, uses this context to give people the best comedy of their lives by surprising them with unforgettable encounters.

Assess how your audience feels and then use every tool you can to change their mood to be more receptive to your comedy.

FUNNIEST-WRITING TIP #16: COMEDY IS AUDIENCE-EXPECTATION MANAGEMENT

*Though only one of the levels on the Comedy Context Pyramid, audience expectations are largely what the skilled comedy writer or performer has learned to manage. Whether it's through the medium they choose, their knowledge of the audience's disposition, or their delivery, they're focused on controlling the audience's expectations at every level. They use every tool at their disposal to make sure the audience is teed up to laugh at whatever comedy they present.*

If you still have an unwilling audience, move up the pyramid and maximize the next contextual element: audience expectation.

If you're in a performance medium, you can create just about any expectation in your audience by the way you behave. If you're in a medium where your material is produced beforehand and only presented it to an audience after it's polished (like a book or a movie), you have less control in the moment.

To control audience expectations, you need to understand the four different categories of comedy audiences:

1. The audience is not expecting humor and doesn't want it.

2. The audience is not expecting humor but would be happy if they encountered some.

3. The audience is expecting humor but skeptical that they'll like it.

4. The audience is expecting humor and know they'll like it.

The category 1 audience is made up of sourpusses who are never going to laugh at anything. They're best left to their misery. Category 4 is the easiest crowd, the one all comedians and comedy writers crave. But it's not the best audience.

Expectations result from the level of surprise that an audience is capable of experiencing. The bigger the surprise you can give your audience, the more satisfying their laughs. The "friendly crowd" of category 4 is already at maximum capacity, so even if they laugh uproariously at the humor, they haven't been very surprised. They'll have a good time, but may not remember it long.

The category with the best leverage is category 2. This type of audience travels the furthest to get their comedy surprise; their mind takes the broadest possible swing from low expectations to a sudden dose of hilarity, giving them a deeply surprising and satisfying laugh. If you can turn a category 2 audience into a category 4 audience, they'll love you forever.

Jokes whispered in the classroom or funeral turn a category 2 audience into a category 4. *The Onion* did the same with its fake newspaper delivered on newsstands. Bill Murray does the same with his notoriety on the street. This kind of category shift in audience expectation is like putty in the hands of the skilled comedy creator. Audiences laugh uncontrollably and remember the surprise for the rest of their lives.

On the set of a comedy TV show with a live audience, the audience is usually made up of fans of the show who came from afar to see the taping. They're a category 4 audience. But the creators nonetheless try to control the context further. They prime the crowd beforehand with a warm-up act that lasts up to an hour. The warm-up act urges the audience to laugh loudly and heartily. The show often doesn't get started until the audience has been sitting in the cold studio for almost two hours. They're beaten down into a category 3 audience. But, because of all the contextualizing (or warm up) the creators do beforehand, they usually have enough goodwill by the time the show starts and their favorite star appears. By that time they switch back to a category 4.

But then the show drags on, and maybe it isn't a very funny episode, or an extra take or two is needed. At this moment the thrill of seeing the celebrity has worn off. The audience drifts back to category 3. Then, suddenly, during the performance, one of the performers flubs a line, or accidentally says something inappropriate, like a swear word, or something the audience knows would never be allowed on TV. Then the real laughter kicks in. The audience's expectations have been so blunted by the constant pressure to laugh that they slip into category 2, laughing only perfunctorily for the soundtrack. But when something happens that they don't expect, they go nuts.

*The Carol Burnett Show* thrived on this phenomenon. The performers were rewarded with such powerful laughs whenever they botched their lines and tried to stifle their laughter on stage that the show began to manufacture these scenarios. *SNL* often does the same.

The final level of the pyramid, directly preceding the release of the comedy, is the delivery. Delivery can be altered in a number of different ways:

**Attitude**

Will your material be funnier if you're smiling, or serious? Typically, the best way to contextualize your humor so that your audience is surprised is to do it with a straight face. However, if you're telling shocking jokes about dismembering people, it might be funnier if you're doing that with a smile.

**Contrast**

Heightening contrast almost always works to make comedy funnier. Andy Kaufman's Elvis impression was funnier because he preceded it with a terrible Jimmy Carter impression. Think about how you can use contrast like Andy Kaufman did to control the context and position the audience to find it funnier.

**Tension**

Audiences love to see tension released. They love to go on an emotional roller coaster ride, even a small one. If you can create a little tension before a joke, your audience will laugh harder when you tell it. For example, after a mobster shoots his target in the head in *The Godfather*, his accomplice says, "Leave the gun. Take the cannoli." The joke is funnier because it immediately follows a murder.

**Discordance**

If your humor makes sense or communicates a truth, try contrasting it with something discordant. If your humor itself is discordant, like in a lot of the Kid Stuff humor category, try contrasting it with a real-world truth to highlight your humor. Dr. Seuss used discordant ideas like made-up words and nonsensical scenarios in his poems to control the context and set readers up to laugh.

**Surprise**

Increasing the amount of surprise the audience experiences will almost always result in a positive shift in context.

**Misplaced focus**

This Funny Filter can be used to control the context of humor by misdirecting the audience to focus on the wrong thing. Anthony Jeselnik uses this technique in his one-liners to amp up the laugh quotient of almost every one of his jokes.

**Tone**

Experiment with different tones in your work. Tones put audiences in whatever mood you want in order to maximize your humor. Sarah Cooper used a belittling and mocking tone to parody Donald Trump in short videos that went viral, setting her apart from other Donald Trump impressionists.

**Timing**

Jerry Seinfeld explains that when he changes the timing in his delivery even slightly, he detects a shift in how big his laughs are. Timing is one of the most important levers in comedy, both as a sledgehammer (telling jokes at the appropriate time), and as a scalpel (how many seconds you wait before delivering a punchline). Controlling all aspects of timing will put your comedy in the best possible light.

### Broadness vs. subtlety

How broad or subtle your humor is will alter its context and affect how audiences perceive it. If you're using Madcap, you usually want to be broad to maximize laughs. (See Chris Farley.) But subtle Madcap thwarts expectations. (See Rowan Atkinson.) Metahumor is often served subtly, à la Bo Burnham. But you change the context when you serve it up broadly, like a lot of the Metahumor jokes used in modern computer-animated movies for kids.

### Props

Props and how they're used can change the context of humor dramatically. In a movie, a line spoken by someone holding a gun will be in a radically different context than one spoken by a character holding a flower.

### Joke construction

Some of the basics of joke construction, like putting the funny part last, eliminating needless words, and playing it straight, all control context. One of the biggest levers of delivery to control context is to comfort the afflicted and afflict the comfortable. Try to afflict the afflicted or comfort the comfortable and you'll quickly experience the power of context.

### Brand

Perhaps the most powerful delivery tool to change the context of humor is brand. Here's the real secret of comedy: established comedy brands get audiences' laughs most reliably. They get them without trying. A brand's audience is category 4. They know and love the brand, and they're primed to like whatever comedy the brand produces. It's not often the quality of the jokes that gets the laughs, it's the audience's recognition and trust of a brand.

A joke told by Will Ferrell, a known brand, will get far bigger laughs than the same joke uttered by someone you meet on a bus. If a fan sees enough episodes of *Family Guy* to decide they like it, they'll watch it and keep watching it even if it's a not-so-great episode. Audiences have been conditioned to accept Will Ferrell and *Family Guy*'s status as legitimate sources of comedy.

Comedy audiences don't think very hard. And they like having short-cuts so that they don't have to think any harder. This fact is what gives context its power, especially when it comes to brand.

There's yet another major way to control context through delivery, but it requires its own chapter.

CHAPTER 14 ACTION STEPS:

*1. Start using the Context Pyramid to be sure you're controlling the context of your comedy.*

*2. Experiment with different ways to change the context of your work to set it up for maximum laughs.*

# NO MORE STAGE FRIGHT

A spotlight hits the empty stage. The emcee steps out and the crowd politely applauds. A few of the emcee's jokes don't connect.

You watch from behind a curtain just off stage. You get a distinct, terrifying feeling in your gut: this is a tough crowd.

The emcee seems to agree. He rushes through his opening. He wants to get off stage as quickly as he can. So he moves things along and begins introducing the next performer: you. You feel a strong burst of butterflies in your stomach. To wrap up his not-so-great introduction, he says, "so please welcome to the stage. . ." mispronounces your name, waves a hand in your direction, and then steps aside.

The stage is all yours.

You walk toward a blinding light and a dark mass of people you can't quite make out. There's a smattering of applause that ends a lot sooner than you expect. Your legs feel weak. A trickle of sweat drips under your arm. Your hands are clammy. Your knees are shaking. Your heart is racing.

You can't catch your breath. Is the room spinning? Are you going to faint?!

Most people call it stage fright. Scientists call it "the fight-or-flight stress response," our instinctive reaction to stressful stimuli. Call it what you want, it's a comedy killer.

And it's not just a fear of the stage that triggers this response. Leading a writers' room or having an important conversation with just one person, especially someone you want to impress, can be equally paralyzing, especially if your presentation involves an attempt to say something funny.

Some of us even feel stage fright when we're all alone, staring at a blank sheet of paper, charged with the daunting task of jotting down a funny idea.

What we all lack in those moments is one thing: confidence.

Confidence is one of the most important ingredients in comedy. A joke delivered to an audience with confidence is met with laughs. The same joke delivered without confidence is met with awkward silence.

If you don't have confidence, very little of what you say or do will be perceived as funny. If you have an abundance of confidence, you'll feel like you can do no wrong. Everything you say and do will seem to get laughs.

Confidence is like a cheat, a shortcut to comedy success. In more practical terms, it's a high-leverage tool that comedians and comedy writers use to control the context of their humor at the delivery stage, and it makes them a lot funnier.

*How to Write Funny*, the first book in this series, included techniques for facing the blank page with confidence. But what about performing publicly or running a writers' room?

If the prospect of speaking in front of a group of people terrifies you, you might be comforted to know that you're not alone. We've all felt the terrible feeling of stage fright. You've probably heard that stage fright consistently ranks as most people's number-one fear. Coming in lower on the list are things like death and the loss of a child.

Why is facing a crowd of people so deeply and universally terrifying, when at least on the surface, it's not dangerous to us in any way?

To understand the answer to this question, you need to understand two things about your brain. First, your brain reacts to stimuli the same way whether real or imagined. If you imagine being in a happy place, your brain will release endorphins and other "feel good" hormones just as it would if you were actually in a real happy location. By the same token, if you imagine a worst-case scenario, your brain will release stress hormones just as it would if you were truly in a worst-case scenario. Your brain doesn't care what's real and what's fantasy—it doesn't know the difference. It runs the same script regardless.

Second, we're little more than glorified puppets acting out the unconscious and unreasonable commands of our chimp and lizard brains. We may think we're rational human beings, but more often than not, we use the "higher" reasoning function of the uniquely human parts of our brains merely to rationalize our mammalian and reptilian behavior.

Modern life presents a Pandora's box of subtle and complex problems that our chimp and lizard brains don't recognize and aren't equipped to handle. When we face these strange new challenges, our frontal cortex is out of its depth. But instead of doing nothing, it handles every problem as best it can, using the limited mammalian or reptilian tools at its disposal. It steps up, well-intentioned, and resorts to clumsy, lower-brain responses to handle situations that would probably go a lot better with a more nuanced approach.

Stage fright, for example, runs through all three levels of our brains like an electric shock. The frontal cortex uses its power of abstract thought to imagine a worst-case scenario. It paints a picture of you as a stumbling, inarticulate performer, it imagines a hostile crowd, or some even worse embarrassment. It dwells on everything that could possibly go wrong.

The mammalian brain offers up deeper insecurities. It has no reference for stepping in front of a crowd of strangers to tell jokes. Your brain evolved on the African savannah, where we likely knew all of our fellow tribe members like family. So your brain gives you the closest reference it has: standing before a sea of hostiles—maybe members of your tribe passing judgement on you, maybe members of an enemy tribe.

Once this ordeal has been imagined, we conclude that the consequences could be fatal. Since we imagine our survival is now at stake, our brain accepts this fantasy as reality. The reptilian brain steps up and triggers the fight-or-flight stress response, flooding you with adrenaline to fend for yourself as you face this angry mob.

The fight-or-flight stress response gives us poor choices. In polite society, we usually can't fight or flee, which leaves us with a third option: we freeze.

Here's the good news: Telling a joke, in most cases, is not going to kill you. The trick is convincing your brain of this fact. You have to convince your brain that you haven't been put on trial, you're not being ejected from the tribe, and these aren't your enemies. You're safe. After the performance you're going home to sleep in your warm bed, still very much alive, surrounded by loved ones.

Trying to control or influence your lower brain with logic and reality is no small task. You can, however, reason with your higher brain, and sometimes all it takes is a little bit of work to keep the dinosaur and the chimp inside you from running amok.

Here are some specific tips for managing the destructive forces of your chimp and lizard ancestors to reduce symptoms of stage fright and present yourself at your calm and confident best:

### Concentrate on a best-case scenario

If you imagine a best-case scenario instead of a worst-case scenario, your brain will give you hope instead of terror, which will put you in a better state to perform. By contrast, if you imagine a worst-case scenario, you'll be mired in the fight-or-fight stress response and face a continuing struggle to keep stressful feelings under control.

Visualize success and truly feel it happening. Experience the sights, sounds, and other sensations of succeeding. Talk to yourself. Instead of saying, "I can't do this," say, "I will ace this!" This self-talk will pump your brain with happy hormones instead of stress hormones, and drastically reduce your feelings of stage fright.

Let your imagination run wild. What's the best thing that could happen after you perform? Imagine it, and enjoy the results of a successful performance in advance. Imagine a roaring standing ovation, accolades, and roses tossed on stage. Imagine you get crowd-surfed.

### When you face the fight-or-flight response, choose fight

Handle stage fright by at least choosing one or the other: fight or flight. Choosing one is healthier than doing nothing (freezing). Using adrenaline to power either a bold fight or a fast escape is healthy and energizing. It's what adrenaline is meant to do. Its job is to give you increased awareness, heightened mental acuity, and energy in a do-or-die moment. Use it!

Frame your presentation as a personal challenge, and then decide to stand up and face it. The antidote to fear is bravery. Often the mere act of consciously deciding to be brave and facing a situation—even before you actually do so—can give you enough confidence to "fight." You'll channel your adrenaline into confidence, creating the most resourceful possible state.

### Use the A-B-C-D-E trick

Another method for beating back your destructive lower-brain impulses, and thereby conquering stage fright, comes from cognitive behavioral therapy. It's the A-B-C-D-E trick. All you need to remember is the first five letters of the alphabet to put your frontal cortex squarely in the driver's seat. At the moment you're feeling stage fright, talk yourself through these steps and answer the questions honestly:

A. What's the <u>A</u>dversity I'm facing? Possible answer: "I'm scared to perform in front of this audience."

B. What does this adversity cause me to <u>B</u>elieve? Answer with your worst-case scenario: "I am a terrible, unattractive presenter. I will fail. My life will be ruined," etc.

C. What is the <u>C</u>onsequence of this belief? Answer honestly: "It makes me feel terrible. It makes me want to give up and go hide. It gives me a bellyache. It makes me feel like a total failure."

D. How would you <u>D</u>ispute this irrational belief? Answer with your most rational, higher-brain voice, your inner therapist: "Of course I know my life will not be over. The audience actually wants to hear what I have to say. I'll probably do fine. What's the big deal? No one's going to hurt me. My family and friends will still love me afterwards. I'll do my best and be proud."

E. How <u>E</u>nergized do you feel now, after disputing your irrational belief? Answer honestly: "I feel a little less scared now!"

The A-B-C-D-E trick resets your brain, and, if done often, trains it to think more positively.

### Pretend to have confidence

"Fake It Till You Make It" (Funniest-Writing Tip #7) is a platitude that works. When you pretend to be confident, your physiology sends a signal to your brain that everything is okay. Your brain responds appropriately, and your body is calmed. This can minimize the fight-or-flight response.

Pretending to have confidence can be difficult, especially if you're physically trembling. But your physiology is an important tool. You don't have to sustain the effort for long. Like a rocketship, you only need to produce enough confidence to get you off the ground. Once you've broken through the atmosphere and used your pretend confidence to step on stage and tell a joke or two, you have momentum. And once you have momentum, you have real confidence, and you can now soar into outer space.

### Brand the feeling, not yourself

Admitting aloud that you're feeling afraid to perform can often help conquer stage fright. But avoid labeling yourself. When you say, "I'm a person who gets stage fright," or "I am not a confident person," or "I can't speak in front of people," you make these qualities a permanent fixture of who you are, which disempowers you. If you say these things enough, you'll start to believe them, and you'll become limited by this mental cage you've built. Instead, label your feelings as temporary. Give your brain the clear signal that you are not inherently ill-equipped to handle the adversity. When you tell yourself, "I admit I'm a little afraid right now, but I'm going to do my best" or "I'm really nervous about this upcoming performance, but I'm still going to try," you give yourself an opening to become confident.

### Be self-deprecating

Talking about how great you are is not very appealing. Make fun of yourself. Don't take yourself seriously. A self-deprecating attitude will not only bolster your confidence, it will encourage the audience to perceive you as a funnier, more appealing person. You'll fall on your face sometimes, which is okay. Laugh it off.

### Ignore your Editor brain

Turn off your Editor brain and let yourself be a Clown. The Editor will surely tell you that you're not good enough. Learn to ignore that voice when performing. That's no time to be an Editor! Rehearse if possible, but then, when the time comes to perform, trust your playful side to deliver without judgment by your Editor.

### Remember that your feelings are normal

Stage fright is something everyone experiences. Before you're on stage, simply reminding yourself that you're just like everyone else can help calm you.

### Prepare

One of the best ways to defeat stage fright is to prepare. Practice your routine in front of a mirror. Video yourself and then analyze the video for flaws. Video yourself again until you like what you see.

Next, get in front of a test audience. Start with an audience made up of a friend or two. Then try a larger group of friends. Work your way up to an open-mic night at a comedy club.

### Realize that bombing can't hurt you

Let's say your worst-case scenario really happens. So what? Every successful comedian has bombed. For many, it's an important crucible that they need to experience. It teaches them that the thing they feared most, totally failing in front of a crowd, didn't hurt them in the least. Most of them look back on the experience and laugh. Audiences have seen bad performances before. Jay Leno wasn't destroyed after he bombed, and you won't be either. In fact, bombing will help you. You'll learn from it, and it will make you more confident.

### Bomb

Get on stage at an open-mic night in front of a drunk or hostile crowd and bomb. Then laugh it off. You don't know those people. Let them boo you. Who cares? Walk off the stage proudly, as if you've just performed a necessary experiment. Then ask yourself, "Am I hurt?" "Do my family and friends still love me?" Chances are, the answer to both those questions will be "yes."

After you bomb, your next performance will be better. You'll be more confident because you've been through the worst-case scenario and survived. You'll learn that speaking publicly can't hurt you. Every performance afterwards will build your confidence further.

### Focus on your audience

Most stage fright comes from being self-conscious, which comes from focusing on yourself instead of others. Your performance is not about you. It's about your audience, and how entertained they're going to be.

Your audience wants to see you. That's why they're here. Ask yourself, "What do they want? What would amuse them?" Ask questions of them to draw them to you. Do crowd work and ask about them. If possible, make friends with someone in the crowd before you perform.

### Breathe

The physical manifestations of stage fright are aggravated when you're short of breath. Take the time to get in a few good, long breaths, in through the nose, out through the mouth.

**Be passionate**

Nobody likes a lackluster performer. Give it your all and speak with passion about whatever you're saying.

> THE SOUND OF YOUR VOICE
>
> *When you perform, speak clearly and directly. Don't mumble. Alter your volume and pace to give variety to the jokes you're telling. Vary other qualities of your performance to keep things interesting: tonality, body language, and the length of pauses all work together to provide the kind of dynamic performances audiences want.*

**Be genuine**

Nobody likes an act. Be comfortable in your own skin and speak from your heart. Doing this will lead to confidence. If you're authentic, you'll have less fear of doing something "wrong." Use your own style; don't try to imitate someone else's.

Confidence in comedy is critical, but it's not a cure-all. Crazy comedic characters like Ace Ventura or Austin Powers have unstoppable confidence, and so do outgoing toddlers who say whatever is on their mind. These characters sing, dance, and tell jokes without any fear of bombing. It's a wonderful quality, but it can wear thin for the audience. Overly confident characters can turn from charming to annoying very quickly. Often, they're being laughed at, not with.

Confidence by itself can get you these kinds of laughs if you want them. But used wisely, and in combination with the other techniques in this book—as well as with great material—you can avoid annoying audiences and truly shine as a confident, cool, and collected comedian.

CHAPTER 15 ACTION STEP

*If you've never gotten on stage to perform comedy, try it. It will make you a better writer, and it will make you a more confident person.*

# 16

# GO NUTS

Congratulations! You've made your way through the first three books in the *How to Write Funny* series. You now have so much know-how about comedy writing swimming around in your brain that you can go off and create enough top-notch comedy to fill the Internet and every other medium for the rest of time.

In these pages, I imparted everything you need to know to craft humor that will be beloved by audiences, that will truly be the funniest possible comedy. You're armed and expertly equipped to be a great comedy writer.

Still, struggling comedy writers—and professionals—continue to tell me that comedy writing can't be taught, that you either "have it or you don't." I addressed this myth in the previous book in this series, but in closing I want to drive the point home so there's no mistaking what makes a great comedy writer.

It takes three things to become a great comedy writer. They're listed here in order of least importance:

### 1. Talent

As science is finding, raw natural talent is a myth. Geoff Colvin elucidates this new thinking in his excellent book, *Talent Is Overrated*. Yet sometimes we encounter people in comedy who seem, for lack of a better word, "talented." They have no professional experience yet seem incredibly funny.

These naturally funny people weren't born with this ability. We're all born pretty serious. They learned it growing up either from their families, friends, or from studying other comedy.

Despite the fact that they weren't born with any special gift for comedy, these people nonetheless worked at it, they picked up some skill, and so we call them "talented."

formula for comedy talent

$$P + S = T$$

I encountered one such person in Madison, Wisconsin, when I was trying to build *The Onion* into a world-class humor publication. His name was Gene, and he worked at the Radio Shack on Henry Street. He was sharp and funny and always cracked me up when I went into the store. I offered him a job writing for *The Onion*. He turned me down.

Where is Gene now? I don't know. But I haven't seen him on the comedy scene, and as far as I know he never pursued it as a profession. His talent did nothing for him.

I found other people like Gene who accepted jobs writing for *The Onion*. Sometimes people who have developed natural gifts rest on their laurels. They often don't go far without one of the other two essential qualities.

So, if talent is all you have, I wouldn't bet on your becoming a great comedy writer.

---

Funniest-Writing Tip #17: Have Fun

*An important ingredient in all humor, one often overlooked by serious and obsessed comedy hopefuls, is an element of fun. Audiences smell a sense of fun in a work of comedy the way a dog can smell fear. And they like it. If your comedy comes off as too calculated, too labored over, or too careful, audiences will sense that something is missing. They don't consciously realize that they want a sense of fun in their comedy, but they can feel when it's not there, and it deadens the entertainment for them. If you have fun when you create your comedy, the audience will sense that you love what you're doing, and this sense will inspire them to love it too.*

---

## 2. Skill development

Peak performance experts now acknowledge that training and skill development are critical to becoming great in any discipline. Comedy is no exception. I've seen countless people apply themselves and learn comedy, often starting with no experience. Taking classes from me, or trying desperately to get a job working for me at *The Onion* and elsewhere, people who didn't seem to possess much natural talent nonetheless worked hard and learned how to do it. Many of these people are now successful comedy professionals.

People who have a little bit of natural talent and who don't merely rest on their laurels but apply themselves and learn some skill go far fast. If you cultivate some innate gifts and you also develop your skills, I give you a fair chance to become great, but it's by no means a guaranteed outcome.

Some people who have natural talent who also commit to developing their skills nonetheless fail to become great comedy writers. They fail because they don't have the third quality.

### 3. Persistence

People without persistence eventually get lazy or disinterested and give up trying. Comedy is merely a passing interest for them.

Meanwhile, other people with no ear for comedy—no "talent" as well as no skill—start raw and unfunny. They get the comedy bug and they persist. These people always succeed.

People who have no other quality but persistence are the ones I bet on. They become great every time.

So how do you get persistence?

Most comedy writers are driven by a powerful engine inside them. They not only love comedy, they need it. If you want to persist at doing comedy like them, there's only one way: you have to love it. You have to love it so much that you become obsessed with it.

Does comedy feel like a slog to you? Are you disappointed that you're not great yet? There are plenty of these kinds of feelings to go around in comedy, and if the weight of disappointment is too much for you and makes you want to quit, you should quit. Comedy is probably not for you.

But if you love comedy, you'll never quit. You can't! And therefore you can't fail. Most professional comedy writers did comedy for free before they ever got paid for it. And they'd do it for free again if they ever stopped making money at it. They have no choice. They love it.

Maybe loving comedy is what people mean when they say "you're either born with it or you're not." Maybe what they mean is that the people who love comedy from an early age are the ones who become great. When you love something, whether you have any natural gift for it or not, you do it obsessively, and you get good at it. Eventually you develop skills. Ultimately you become great. People start calling you "a great talent." Maybe even a "genius."

If you didn't grow up loving comedy, you can fall in love with it later in life. You can fall in love with comedy and get obsessed at any age.

So, I lied earlier. Becoming a great comedy writer only takes one thing: persistence. Talent and skill development are merely things you pick up along the way if you're persistent.

If you've read all the *How to Write Funny* books, I suspect you're someone who loves comedy. I'm glad. That means you don't need me to tell you to keep doing it. You don't need me to tell you to practice writing jokes and short pieces on your own. You don't need me to tell you to work with a group to amp up your quality. You'll do it anyway. You have to. Because you love it.

> GO FURTHER
>
> *Visit HowtoWriteFunny.com for more resources to improve your comedy writing. Check out the courses page and take a workshop or online class with me. Listen to the How to Write Funny podcast, where I interview successful comedy professionals about how and why they do what they do. Read blog articles. Download free ebooks and my Joke-writing Cheat Sheet.*

Comedy can be a competitive field, filled with a lot of bitterness and jealousy. Don't succumb to it. Let your love for comedy envelop everyone. Become a part of the comedy community where you live. Celebrate your contemporaries' greatness. Inspire other comedy writers with your obsession. Be a Johnny Appleseed of comedy. We all want more laughter in the world, so let's spread it.

CHAPTER 16 ACTION STEP

*Have fun!*

## Acknowledgments

This book owes its existence and the depth of its contents to the following people:

Everyone who took my "Writing with *The Onion*" courses at The Second City Training Center in Chicago and online.

Everyone who read and appreciated *How to Write Funny,* which served as the basis of the Second City curriculum, and asked me to write a book based on the second level of the courses, which became *How to Write Funnier.*

Those students who took level three of the "Writing with *The Onion*" program, "Advanced Writing with *The Onion*." Many of their thoughts, insights, trials, and errors went into the writing of this book.

Tommy Schneider and Billy Worley, who collectively made me realize the importance of the Glue.

All the writers and other staff who worked with me at *The Onion.* All the writers and other staff who worked with me on my post-*Onion* humor books, *Trump's America: Buy This Book and Mexico Will Pay for It* and *Welcome to the Future Which Is Mine*. All the creative professionals I worked with creating The Onion Radio News, audiobooks for *Our Dumb Century*, *Our Dumb World*, *The Book of Known Knowledge*, and *Trump's America*. Everyone I worked with on *Bad Meat* and *Spaceman*, and all the short films I've made. My two friends Peter Hilleren and Keith Webster, for our formative group-writing experiences. I drew heavily from all of these projects and the lessons I learned from them.

Jaya Chatterjee for excellent proofing, Madeline Schmidt for superb marketing, and all the members of this book's "street team."

Holly Schwartz and Alan Gleeson for their stellar work producing the audiobook version.

Finally, and most importantly, my family and friends, who've come to expect me to be working at all times, especially Dandelion Benson and Brooke Washington, who celebrate that reality.

What's the single biggest mistake you make every day writing comedy?

What are the specific lines you have to avoid or you'll absolutely tank your writing?

How do you stay on top of the latest pitfalls in the fast-changing world of comedy writing?

Printed in Great Britain
by Amazon

45714527R00081